THE
CREDIT CODE

JAE ISAIAH

TABLE OF CONTENTS

Beginner's Guide to Credit!..4
What's Your Credit..8
Score..8
A Complete Guide to Your Credit Score......................10
How to Increase Your Credit Scores 16
Credit Scores - How Do They Work?.............................22
8 Ways To Boost Your Credit Score 28
How To Build Credit Without a Credit Card? 34
A Guide to Your Credit Rating...38
5 Harmful Credit Report Myths 47
The History of Credit and Your Credit Report History................52
Terminology You Need to Know to Understand Your Credit Report..61
How To Avoid Mistakes On Your Credit Report.........67
How To Fix A Negative Credit Report In JUST 3 Simple Steps....74
Credit Rating! What Do You Know About It?.............78
Credit Ratings..83
Credit Freeze - How To Do It and What It Does.........87
Credit Freeze, Fraud and You 89
Identity Theft..92
The 5 C's of Credit 94
Financial Freedom 99
Start your journey to Financial Freedom 110
The 6 Keys to Financial Freedom 118

AUTHORS NOTE !!!

The purpose of writing this book was to help everyone out there, learn the importance of CREDIT and what it takes to achieve success and to both, Avoid and Solve the problems. This book will help you to Understand Credit in the easiest possible way and will guide you to increase

Your credit score as it is one of the problems that affect millions of people today. My work about this topic is to make difference in someone's life by helping them achieve Financial freedom by teaching them what I've learned in my journey.

I hope You'll love the book and appreciate the effort.

Thank you!

BEGINNER'S GUIDE TO CREDIT!

I remember back when I was 18, completely oblivious to the concept of credit, If only I had known then what I know now about credit , My life would have been quite different alot earlier. At 29, I started my journey of learning .So Here I am Writing this short guideline to give you the most important ideas on how you can build a solid credit rating, even if you have to do it from scratch!!

Everyone has to start somewhere, whether you are 18, or even 30 like I was, there is no better time to just start thinking about your financial future. Chances are, your credit score will come to play during some point down your financial-life road. And when that time comes, you had better have some concept of credit and how it can help you, or else you might find yourself unable to qualify for much of anything.

First of all, Even if you are just starting , don't worry! It will take some time, but eventually you will be able to qualify for the bigger things like a car or a mortgage. The first thing you need to do is establish your credit and the easiest way to do this is to get a credit card issued by your bank.Chances are, If you already have an account, then the bank won't have any problem with issuing a card to one of it's current clients. But If you don't already have a checking account, you can get a new one easily! There are a ton of great banks out there that issue free checking accounts with check cards to new customers. But take a note! **A check card** or **ATM card** isn't the same as a **Credit card**! With these you are simply withdrawing the money that you already have in your checking or other accounts. A credit card is very different...

A credit card is actually a right given to you by your lender to borrow a set amount of money from them. You might be shocked to find out that the only card you can get when you are first starting out comes with an outrageous interest rate. Sometimes as high as 15-25%. But don't fret... as long as you pay off your balance every month, those interest rates will be easier to swallow, and you will be eventually able to qualify for a card with a much lower interest rate.

AN IMPORTANT NOTE: In order to have an excellent credit score for lifetime, you need to develop a personal goal, DO NOT EVER make a late payment for anything.I was lucky to have parents who promoted the importance to pay bills on time. There were times when I owed money for a credit card bill, and I was so afraid that the lender would evaluate my bill and ding my credit which will have a negative impact on my credit score, that I stopped borrowing money , just to make sure my credit record stayed clean! I know that seems a little crazy, but trust me, it is extremely important to pay all of your bills on time, even if you have to go out of your way to do it. You will appreciate your diligence down the road.

A WARNING NOTE: Be careful with your spending! It may seem exciting when you first get a credit card with a $1,000 limit, but it can be very dangerous. It is very tempting to pretend that your credit card represents money that you have in the bank. My advice, don't ever spend more than you can pay off in that same month. And if you aren't able to pay off your entire balance in a month, pay more than the minimum requirement. This will help as a booster later.

After you have had your credit card for a while, and feel that you can handle the responsibility, try moving onto one of the major credit card Companies and Try to find one with the lowest interest rate and no annual fee. Don't apply for too many at once! One or two should do just fine. Each time you apply for a C.C., the company will run your credit to see if you will qualify and what should be your spending limit .If you did well in handling your bank C.C., you should have no problem qualifying. The company I like is **Providian**; mostly because they give you a brief snapshot of what your credit score is each month, and as a beginner, you will have to pay attention to what your score is and how it will get affected by your different spending habits. After a while of responsible spending with your new credit cards, your score will really start to move. You'll notice multiple credit card offers from many companies mysteriously start showing up in the mail. Your score will probably be somewhere around 600-650. This isn't a bad credit score, but it could be better. Most likely, it is around this range because of your lack of credit history. As you can see in our Credit overview section, length of credit history accounts for, around 15% of of your overall score.

Another factor that comes into play with your score is the type of credit you have been issued; approx.10% of your score relies on it.You can only build this much credit with your credit cards. Eventually lenders would like to see some other forms of proof that you are responsible with monies borrowed. This is where a personal loan, or a car loan can be helpful. Lenders view this as a different kind of borrowing than from the credit card companies. **In terms of building your credit, these types of loans are great.**

After that, you should see a significant leap in your credit score, and should be able to move onto bigger and better things like a home mortgage loan! Just always make sure you remember the fundamentals**:** **always pay your bills on time, and never spend beyond your means**. With these tips in mind, you will be on your way to making sound financial decisions for life.

WHAT'S YOUR CREDIT SCORE

Everybody is probably aware of the fact that their credit score makes a huge difference while applying for loans. In case, If you have a poor credit score then lending agencies may not consider sanctioning a loan. But If your credit score is above the perfect level then you have a better chance because of your proven track record. But the time has come for you to apply for installment loans regardless how good or bad your credit score is.

Now, the finance market has started offering unsecured and secured installment loans also known as **cash loans bad credit** to all the people who are facing financial troubles. You may be wondering how you could qualify even though you have issues of CCJs, IVAs and bankruptcy and other arrears of paybacks. But these are overlooked now and applicants are being sanctioned cash loans bad credit by financers.

You can apply for either unsecured or secured cash loans depending upon the amount of cash you want to borrow. For Example; if you want to borrow a sum between 5000 to 75000, then it would fall under the **Secure cash loans bad credit** scheme for which you will be required to show some documentation of a property you own, or could be a car or a piece of land which you would be required to pledge as collateral. The interest rate would be much lesser compared with the **Unsecured cash loans bad credit** as this scheme allows you to borrow a sum between 1000 and 25000.

There are a couple of reasons like educational purposes, pending bills, house repairs etc which can be stated while applying for a loan. You must be a valid citizen of the USA holding an active bank account and above 18 years of age to be eligible for the money.

A COMPLETE GUIDE TO YOUR CREDIT SCORE

If you don't know what your credit score is, you should. This is one of the most basic pieces of information, potential creditors use when they decide whether or not, you should qualify for a loan or credit card, for example; Sometimes your credit score is also used as a means to gauge your reliability, as a potential employee, when you apply for certain jobs, and for other important situations. For this reason, it's very important not just to know what your credit score is, but also to know how to use it in your favour.

Your Credit Score - Defined

It should be noted, first of all, that the most important type of credit score is something known as the FICO score. **"FICO"** stands for "Fair Isaac Corporation." The Fair Isaac Corporation simply developed a process whereby your credit score is calculated based upon a number of factors, including such factors as how reliable you are with payments (are they on time?), how much debt you owe, whether or not you've defaulted on a loan or credit card, and so on. It should be noted that there ARE other so-called "credit score" calculations out there, but the only one most people pay attention to, is the FICO score. All three major credit bureaus (**Experian, TransUnion, and Equifax**) use FICO scores on their reports. FICO scores can run anywhere from 300 to 850, with the average in the United States being between about 600 to the maximum, 850. You should also note that many lenders will not even consider lending money to people with scores below about 600.

Who are Credit Reference Agencies?

These are commercial companies which collect information or data from a number of sources such as the electoral roll, county court judgments and other financial institutions. This information is sold to lenders which help them in their evaluation of your credit worthiness or how much they are willing to lend you, if at all they will. There are three credit reference agencies in the United Kingdom, these are: Equifax, Experian and Call Credit

Getting Your Credit Score

There are lots of companies out there these days, touting services that will **"watch"** your credit report for you and report suspicious activity. However, you don't need to spend a lot of money to simply pull your credit report from each of the three major agencies (again, Experian, TransUnion or Equifax). If you have a very common name, you've been a victim of identity theft in the past, and/or you have a LOT of activity going on continually in your credit history, one of these services may be useful. However, if you don't, then simply pulling your credit report (from all three bureaus) every six months to every year so that you can check activity should be sufficient.

The federal government supplies every consumer with a free credit report once year from each of the three credit bureaus. To claim yours, go to **Annualcreditreport.com**. It should be noted that this free credit report is not going to give you, your FICO score, so that's something you have to buy; it's pretty inexpensive to do so, though, and you should only have to do it once a year. For that, you can go to **my FICO.com** and pay a small fee for just one of the credit scores; some people say the TransUnion is the most commonly used of the credit bureaus, but any of the three should do.

Okay, You Know Your Credit Score; Now What?

Once you've determined what your credit score is and have your credit reports in hand, take a look at your credit score and see where you compare to the rest of the country. Have you had difficulty with finances in the past? This could mean that your credit score is less than it should be. However, you also need to take a look at what's on your credit report itself. Is there activity you don't recognize as yours?

Now, first of all, don't panic. It could mean identity theft, true, but likely not. Credit bureaus are notorious for making errors on credit reports, and by law, they have to fix them. Therefore, make note of anything that's not yours, write the credit bureau in question noting these errors (for best results, it's often a good idea to send your letter by registered mail so that you have a record that they received it), and guess what? They have to investigate every single incident and have the creditor in question respond. If it's found not to be yours, or if the creditor does not respond, they have to drop it off of your credit report, usually within 60 days. This takes care of these types of errors. However, pull your credit report again in six months and make sure none of them have simply "**come back**." Sometimes this happens and it takes a time or two for these types of things to drop off of your credit report. Write to the credit bureaus again (enclosing a copy of your previous letter so that they know you've contacted them before) and demand (nicely, but do absolutely demand) that these errors be removed.

Now, onto **negative things on your credit report** that are yours. If you've had a financial difficult, then many of your creditors would have reported that you're late on payments or have missed them; accounts, that you have defaulted on, will be on the report too.

Again, if this is you, don't panic. However, you do have to be responsible for your past behavior and take care of your mistakes. One of the first things you need to be aware of is that NO ONE can simply "**fix**" your credit report for you if the negative information is indeed yours. Negative information is something that you're going to have to take care of or that in some cases will simply "**age off**" your credit report in several years.

Here's what you do; If you've had financial troubles and had difficulty paying bills in the past, clean up your act NOW and begin to be responsible. Why? Because time here is a panacea.

Simply replacing "old" irresponsible behavior with "new" responsible behavior is going to improve your credit score by default, over time. That's because "old" irresponsible behavior from the past (beginning by about two years after the irresponsible behavior occurred) doesn't count as much to creditors as your current behavior. So if you're behaving responsibly now and you have been for a while, that's what creditors (and in some cases, employers, etc.) are going to look at.

What this means is that you have to get that clock ticking now. If you're behaving irresponsibly right now, stop. Begin to act responsibly and start paying your bills on time. If one of your major difficulties is credit card debt, STOP using credit cards, Right now. Sit down, figure out a budget, and contact any creditors you've gone into arrears with and set payment arrangements to begin paying that debt off. Pay your main bills first (rent, food, utilities, and so on). Then, put 10% in savings. The rest of your income goes toward debt until it's paid off. There are many systems out there to help you pay off this debt, such as picking the credit card with the lowest amount on it, making minimum payments on all of your other credit cards and then applying the balance of your debt money toward that credit card until it's paid off; then, go onto the next "lowest balance" credit card and do the same thing; make minimum payments toward the other credit cards, put the rest of your debt money toward that credit card, paid off, and then go on to the next one.

Keep checking your credit score every six months or so and you should see it begin to creep up. Again, within about two years, old behavior (even **"bad" behavior**) does not have as much of an impact on your credit score as current behavior does. So any mistakes you've made in the past shouldn't have much of an impact on you after a certain amount of time has passed.

A note about credit cards: Yes, they're handy, and in some cases people say you "must" have them simply to live. Now, that's not true, but if you want a credit card that's going to help you reestablish your credit score and you want the convenience of credit card but you can't get one (or you don't want the risk of one), you can start with something called a **"secured" credit card**. A secured credit card works like a regular credit card except that you make a deposit with the lending institution for the exact credit line of that credit card. You help reestablish your credit history by making payments on that credit card on time, too (pay off the full balance every month), but the difference is, if you default on that credit card, the lending institution simply takes the money out of your deposit and pays itself back the money it "lent" you on the credit card purchase. It's meant as a tool to help you learn to use credit wisely again, not to simply fall back into old habits that got you into trouble in the first place.

If your credit score is good now, great. If it's not, don't panic. You can reestablish a good credit history (and therefore credit score) once again by simply replacing **"bad" behavior** with **"good" behavior** financially, so that you'll be on the path to financial health once again.

HOW TO INCREASE YOUR CREDIT SCORES

Since the score is based on information - positive and negative - in a consumer's credit report, incorrect information - especially if that information is derogatory as defined by the model - can lead to **a lower-than- warranted score**. But, with the system now in place, correcting and deleting negative and incorrect information can take weeks, and even after the information is corrected by the creditor in its own files, the creditor often takes weeks more to report, via magnetic tape, the new, more-positive information to the credit repository (of which there are three: Trans Union, Experian - formerly TRW - and Equifax, which dominates here in North Carolina). But congressional, regulatory, and consumer pressure are coming to bear on this cumbersome, paper-based "corrections" system. Recently a credit industry official told me the credit bureaus - which are local that sell reports compiled by the three large repositories and which have the most direct contact with consumers - are negotiating with the repositories to be able to help consumers make changes faster. Under the proposal, the local bureau would check out consumer complaints directly with the creditor and, if the creditor confirms that the information is, indeed, incorrect, the bureau will be able to change the so-called **"raw"** credit file directly with all three of the repositories without waiting for the creditor to check out the complaint, update its files, and then send the updated information to the repository. A process that, as I noted, can take weeks - long enough to kill a deal. This is a major development. With the raw file changed, a new, possibly higher, score can be quickly generated, a deal rescued, and consumer and congressional concerns can be addressed.

Additionally, the three repositories continue to attempt to cooperate with one another, in theory sharing any updated, corrected information about consumers to insure their files are as accurate as possible. (But, just to be safe, consumers should make corrections with all three repositories directly – don't assume anything; they are, after all, competitors.) The three repositories each use a different version of the Fair, Isaacs scoring model, but the model has been adjusted and weighted, so, theoretically, if all three had the very same information on you, your three scores would be identical. (A score of 640 at one repository would represent the same odds as a 640 at either of the other repositories, according the Fair Isaacs.) Of course, not all creditors report to all three repositories, so, even with adjustments, consumers can sometimes end up with three quite-different scores. While it is true that, in theory, you can have great credit with one repository and bad credit with another, I have rarely, if ever, seen that happen, although I have seen some pretty wildly varying scores. In a few cases I have seen borrowers with scores that vary by 100 points or more. To combat this variance, the mortgage industry usually uses the middle score, but that can be of little comfort to a borrower if he/she has scores of 550, 570 and 700, and the interest rate for a borrower with a 570 score is two points higher than for a borrower who has a 700 score. Still, keep in mind that this situation is rare. A borrower with good credit would, for example, have scores something like 685, 702, and 710.

Other new developments include outreach efforts to educate consumers about credit scoring by conducting seminars and sending out publications on the subject, plus efforts to make scores more readily available to consumers. Federal law says consumers do not have a right to see their score, but does not specifically prohibit lenders and creditors from revealing it (the credit report you can purchase from your local credit bureau does not have your scores posted - for now, only reports ordered by creditors have scores). Many in the mortgage industry, who know just enough about credit scoring to be dangerous, wrongly believe they are not allowed to tell you, your score. That may be their company's policy, but the Federal Trade Commission has made it crystal clear that it is illegal to reveal scores to a consumer, and some industry and consumer groups are now coming out in support of release of the scores. I strongly support the release of scores to consumers, so long as the scores are accompanied by information about how the scores are computed (my columns work nicely, I would think), so a number isn't just shoved at a consumer with no context or explanation.

In fact, until recently, Fair, Isaacs has opposed the release of the score to the consumer, fearing that, as the company told me in an e-mail, since "**the nature of credit risk scoring requires that consumers behave normally (and therefore predictable) when managing their credit and if large numbers of consumers receive and misunderstand their credit risk scores, their short-term behavioral changes could harm the predictive accuracy of the scoring model.**" Fair, Isaacs position is that "**the expansion of the credit industry in the 80s and 90s (was) made possible by expanded use of tools like credit scoring,**" so anything that hurts the "**predictive accuracy**" of the model could make credit less-available. I would acknowledge that some might say that making credit less available is a good thing!

The five categories found to be more predictive (with their relative weighting in parentheses) are:

- **Past Payment Performance (35%):** Do you pay your bills on time? The more recent the late payments, the lower you credit score. In fact, a 30 day late payment today hurts more than a bankruptcy five years ago.

- **Credit Utilization (30%):** Have you maxed out your credit lines? Low balances on a few cards are better than high balances on one or two cards. Keeping balances below 30% of the credit line increases your chance for a higher score.

- **Credit History (15%):** The longer your accounts have been open, the better, so surfing for a new lower rate on a credit card and transferring balances can hurt your score.

- **Types of Credit In Use (10%):** Getting a loan at a finance company rather than a bank or credit union lowers your score.

- **Inquiries (10%):** Applying for new credit lowers your score, but multiple inquiries from the same type of creditor - like mortgage companies or car dealers - within 14 days count as only one inquiry. Promotional or administrative inquiries do not count against the score - only those times, that you applied for credit, count.

It's no secret that Fair, Isaacs isn't happy about the relative weightings leaking out, and it contends that the relative ratings above are not necessarily correct. The company, in an e-mail, to me "**...the numbers change over time. That's why we periodically update our models and score cards to account for changes in consumer behaviors, lender policies, etc.**" Well, then, now that we know how a score is computed, how do you go about improving it? Certainly the best way is to pay your bills on time. You should also keep your balances to below 30% of your credit line, and its better to keep some small balances on several cards rather than high balances on one or two. Maintain your accounts for a long period of time. Limit the number of times you apply for credit.

What if you have done all that and there is incorrect derogatory information on your report? Challenge it quickly with the help of a mortgage professional, and insist the creditor to correct the information promptly. It can't hurt to check out your credit report with a mortgage professional a few months before you intend to apply for a mortgage. But, in any case, with the increasing amount of identity theft occurring, you should check your credit report at least once a year anyway.

CREDIT SCORES - HOW DO THEY WORK?

Credit scoring is a complicated process and each of the 3 major credit repositories have their own credit scoring models in place to determine a borrower's credit score. The 3 main credit repositories are Equifax, Experian, and TransUnion. Equifax has credit scores that range from a lowest possible score of 300 and a highest possible score of 850. Experian has a range of 340-820 and TransUnion 150-934. Just like computers have upgraded operating systems over the years such as, Windows 98, Windows 2000, and Windows XP, the credit scoring system versions update periodically also. Not all lenders use the same version or the most updated version when obtaining a credit report and credit score for a borrower. Therefore, this is one reason why you may have varying credit scores between one lender and another.

There are five major components or factors that help to determine your credit score. Roughly 35 percent of your credit score is derived from your payment history, 30 percent from how much you owe compared to how much you have available, 15 percent comes from length of credit history, 10 percent from new credit and recent inquiries, and the final 10 percent comes from various other items such as the mixture of credit you currently have. Next we will discuss each of the five components in further detail and explain the basic principals as to how credit scoring works. This information is to be used only to help educate and as a guide to assist with the basic ideas involved in credit scoring.

Payment History (35%)

Your payment history is the most important factor of credit scoring. Bankruptcies, collection accounts, slow pays and late payments, foreclosures, judgments, and liens can negatively affect your credit score. However, an established history of **on-time payments** and **a clean credit history** will positively impact your credit scores and help to increase them over time. The older any negative credit history or adverse credit factors are, the less they will negatively affect your credit score. Therefore, recent bad history will negatively affect your credit much greater than aged bad credit.

Revolving Credit Balances to Maximum Limits (30%)

The credit scoring models are going to look heavily upon how much revolving credit you have available compared to how much you have used. For credit scoring purposes, having all revolving credit or credit card accounts maxed out to their limits is not a good thing, nor is it going to help better your credit scores. You don't want to pay off all of your revolving credit accounts because that will not show the credit bureaus how well you manage your credit. Your ideal credit ratios should be roughly **20-40 percent**

usage. What this means is that if you have a credit card with a $1000 limit you do not want to max. out the credit card balance, but you would want to maintain a balance between 200 and 400 dollars. If you do realize that you have borrowed more than 50% of your available credit limit on your card or your balance is getting close to your limit, you should either try to pay your balance down to the 40% mark or call your credit card company and see if they are able to raise your limit. The biggest mistake you can make is to let your balance exceed your maximum credit limit. This will negatively affect your credit score a great amount.

Length of Credit History (15%)

The longer and more established your credit history is, the better and more positive of an impact it can make. Someone who pays their bills on time for a 10 year period of time is a much better risk than someone who only has a 1 year history of paying their bills on time, even if they both carry the same credit score. When you pay off credit card accounts do not close them, keep them open and use them periodically in order to continue to build an established length of credit. Closing your accounts can actually have more of a negative affect on your credit score due to limiting the length of time that particular account was open for. **The longer you have established credit accounts, the better it is for you.** It is possible to still have a good credit score with a short credit history; however lenders still may not approve you for optimal financing options due to the lack of history.

New Credit and Inquiries (10%)

The amount of new credit you have opened, will have somewhat of a minor impact on your credit scores. If you have numerous inquiries resulting from applying for a lot of new credit and add many new trade-lines in your credit report, this can have a damaging effect on your credit score. First, because you have a lot of new, un-established accounts. Second, because you have a lot of inquiries with various lenders for various types of financing over a short period of time.

Credit inquiries can affect your credit score, not a ton, but enough to lower your score. This is not to say, don't shop around or don't have more than one firm pull your credit, when looking to buy a car or a home. You definitely should use due diligence and shop between a couple of lenders to make sure you are getting a good deal. When you are comparing quotes however, you should try to do all of your shopping within a 30 day max. period of time. **All inquiries that are made when applying for an auto loan or a mortgage loan are treated as only one inquiry when they are done within a 14 day period of time.** Therefore if you are ever told to not have anyone else pull your credit or else your scores will lower, this has little truth to it. There is only one type of credit inquiry that counts toward your credit score and that is when you are making an application for credit: such as a home loan, auto loan, credit card, etc... When you pull your own credit, a creditor you already have an account with, pulls your credit, and/or a prospective employer pulls your credit, these do not have any impact on your scores. Understanding this can help you make sure that you do not fall victim to all of the urban myths regarding credit inquiries.

Types & Mixture of Credit (10%)

Having a mixture of the various types of credit will have a small impact on your credit scores. For a person, who has a good mixture of credit, such as a home loan, auto loan, 2-4 credit cards and maybe a personal loan this could be deemed **a good mixture of credit** versus a different person who has 15 credit cards and no other credit. The ideal number of credit cards to maintain is 2-4. Also, other types of liabilities are important to have, such as installment loans and a mortgage loan.

"**Knowledge is power**" and the most important step to applying for a loan is to understand **your credit report, your credit scores and how credit scoring works**. It is highly recommended that every person checks their credit report at least once per year to help protect themselves from inaccurate information and from identity theft. You are permitted to obtain a free credit report from each of the three credit repositories, by logging into the annual credit report and following the directions. Report will not contain your credit score. It is also highly recommended that you pull a report from each repository individually when you are utilizing your free annual credit report. If you show you can handle different types of credit at the same time, you are rewarded with a great credit score. By mixing it up, you demonstrate you can manage your credit because you will have short term and long term credit with a fixed payment. As well as a "variable" monthly payment on your credit cards.

Keep these accounts open with a balance of 70% or less and paid on time and you will witness your credit score climb to great heights

In conclusion, your credit is very important and understanding the basics of how your credit scores are obtained is important.

8 WAYS TO BOOST YOUR CREDIT SCORE

1. Deleting Errors in 48 Hours

This is the absolute fastest way to correct errors on your credit report and raise your credit score. However, it can only be done through a mortgage company or a bank. If you apply for a home loan and find errors on your credit report, request the loan officer to conduct a Rapid Re-score. But don't mistake it for the credit clinic tactic of multiple dispute letters.

The Rapid Re-score strategy requires proper paperwork. You need proof that the item is incorrect. It must come from the creditor directly. For example, a letter stating the account is not your account, a letter stating the account was paid satisfactorily, a release of lien, a satisfaction of judgment, a bankruptcy discharge, a letter for deletion of collection account or any relevant evidence.

This is the same documentation a bank or mortgage company would require for the credit accounts anyways. The difference is, now you can improve your credit score and receive a lower interest rate. The results are not guaranteed and will run you about $50 per account.

2. Deleting Negative Credit

This is the infamous area where you've heard of all the scams. Credit repair clinics charge "an arm and a leg" and promise a clean credit report. Sometimes even a new credit profile! People spending hundreds, or even thousands, of dollars for something they can do themselves.

Removing errors is simple. Deleting negative credit that is accurate requires advanced methods. But that is not the scope of this report. So I'll focus on the deleting the negative errors.

Credit report errors easily disappear by using a simple dispute letter. If you have the paperwork proving the error as mentioned above in Rapid Re-score, send copies of that along with the dispute letter. This will make the credit bureau's job easier and you will get faster results.

If you don't have the documentation to prove the error(s), send the dispute letter anyway. According to federal law, the credit bureau's have a "**reasonable time of 30 days**" to validate your claim. They will contact the creditor for verification of your dispute. Then the account will be reported accurately - or deleted. If you're not the do-it-yourself kind of person. Or don't have the time. You could hire someone who is very economical.

3. PiggyBack Someone's Credit

This is a fast and great little credit score booster. But it requires a very trusting relationship. Simply put, **someone else adds you**

to their credit account. For example, when applying for a credit card, you may have seen the section to add a card holder. If your trusting person adds you, their payment history is now reported on your credit report too. If they have perfect credit, now you have a perfect account.

To make this more effective, use an aged account. Imagine if your trusted person has a 10 year old credit card account with a perfect payment history and a balance of only 50% of the credit limit. Wouldn't you love to have this on your credit report? The easy part is your trusted person just calls the credit card company and requests a form to add a cardholder. Once completed and activated, their entire account history and future is now firmly planted on your account. Imagine if you secured 3-5 of these accounts - especially installment accounts. **Your credit score could sky-rocket!**

The challenging part? Finding the trusted person. Since you already have a low credit score and bad credit, how eager will someone be to make you a cardholder? Even your parents don't want you to damage their credit. But, no one says you need to possess the card! In other words, your trusted person could add you as a card holder and never give you the card or PIN or any information. Since the bills and all account information is still mailed to the trusted person's address, you won't know anything about the account. **This scenario could land you many trusted persons.** And you still benefit with a higher credit score.

4. Playing Round Robin

This strategy is one of the oldest credit building techniques around. It used to be accomplished with secured Savings accounts. But now, it's much easier with secured Credit cards. In fact, I've used this method myself.

Here's how it works: Take, 000 (or what you can afford) and get a secured credit card. Once received, get a cash advance of 70% of your credit limit. Get a second secured credit card. Once received, get a cash advance of 70% of your credit limit. Get a third secured credit card. Once received, get a cash advance of 70% of your credit limit.

Open a new checking account with the final cash advance. Use this account only for making payments on your three new credit cards. If you make your payments on time every month, your credit score will increase because you now have three new perfect payment credit cards. (Initially, your credit score might drop a few points due to the rapid, multiple accounts being opened. However, be patient **because within 4 months of no new accounts or any delinquencies of any account, you will see your credit score increase**. Mine increased 60 points in 60 days!!)

5. Pay on Time

This one is quite obvious. But after 12.5 years in the mortgage business, I discovered it still needs repeating. Your creditors were gracious enough to loan you money. Now pay your damn bills! **If you don't, your credit score decreases.** EVEN IF ONLY 30 DAYS LATE!

That's right folks. For some reason people think, "I'm only a few weeks late. What's the big deal?" Well, for the loan company, if you pay late but consistent, they make a lot more money with late fees and more interest (if a simple interest loan). For you, your credit score is damaged. If you think long-term and credit score, I'm certain you would not have a cavalier attitude

6. Pay Down Debts

This seems like an obvious method, doesn't it? But it is not as transparent as you might think. Remember, we're playing with high-level statistics and probabilities which evaluates and forecasts trends in your behavior. Here's what you do...

Never pay off your revolving debt in it's entirety! Isn't that a surprise? Think about it. Your credit score is a reflection of your ability to manage your credit. Paying off your debt is not managing your debt. If you have a zero balance, how can you manage it? You don't. It no longer exists. And you cannot manage what does not exist, right? Therefore, in terms of credit score, you have demonstrated your ability to swiftly pay off accounts to avoid managing them. Thus, slightly decreasing your credit score.

One exception, of course, is if you're over extended to begin with. Pay off what's necessary to make your credit profile look great. Then manage the remaining credit.

7. No New Credit

You must be vigilant in your credit behavior if you want the best credit score. Therefore, **do not get any new credit unless it is absolutely necessary.** Each time you apply for credit, an inquiry is added to your report. This usually drops your credit score slightly. When you have fresh credit, there is no track record how you will manage (or pay) this account. Therefore, it's a higher risk which results in a minor drop in your credit score. Remember, your credit score is about risk assessment.

Here's what you do: obtain credit for your housing, transportation, college or continued education and 3-5 credit cards. That's really all you need for personal credit. **If you want more credit, request a credit limit increase on your current cards rather than apply for new ones.**

8. Don't File Bankruptcy or Foreclosure

Here's the most obvious advice: Don't file for bankruptcy or foreclosure. **These stay on your credit report for 10 years and always decrease your credit score.** The older the bankruptcy or foreclosure account becomes, coupled with re-built credit history, the less of an impact they play on your credit score.

Contrary to popular beliefs, you can legally delete a bankruptcy and foreclosure. It's not easy. But it's possible. See the advanced methods for that solution.

HOW TO BUILD CREDIT WITHOUT A CREDIT CARD?

There are many people in this world that have the ability to build credit wisely without resorting to a credit card. Their chances of getting credit approved are high and this is the reason they prove the notion wrong that credit cards are the only source of credit . Now the obvious question comes to mind and that is - How is it possible to build credit without credit card?

In order to successfully build credits without a credit card, the first and foremost thing that you should understand is that what are the lenders searching for. Your FICO score is the first step to get credit and based on this score these lenders determine whether they will lend you the credit. There are other factors that they take into consideration when they are about to determine whether to sanction you the credit or not. They have been underlined below:

1. Lenders seem to see bank accounts as a sign of stability. Banks accounts do not require credit to open and this is the reason why you can resort to this simple step by opening a checking account in your local branch. You information does not get reported to the credit bureau and your account becomes a vital source of credibility for the lenders to decide on to give you the loan or not.

The moment you are opening a checking account in a local branch you are sending out a positive message to the lender that you have the ability to manage money. The lenders can take information and determine whether you are a credit risk or not. In addition to this, if you maintain a positive relationship with the bank your chances of getting the credit approved are high as this carried a lot of weight when lenders approach the bank to acquire information. The bank will value your business and this will work in your favor.

You also have another option where you can open a joint credit card account. This can be done with someone but you must keep in mind the point that by opening this account you are making the other person liable for credit too.

2. A clean employment history will also help lenders determine the sanction of credit to you. They look into your work consistency and your stability to hold on to jobs. This increases your likelihood of getting credit approved faster.

3. The history of your residence is also taken into account and lenders will also determine the frequency of your moves and your ability to stay in one place for a long time. The stability of your residence carries weight and if you are the owner of a home even jointly with your spouse the chances of getting your credit approved are high.

4. You can also use credit like cards like a secured card or a change card. A secure card can be obtained by making a deposit with the credit union or the issuing bank and receiving a card that

has a specified credit limit. The procedure is similar to that of a prepaid card however you have to ensure that the lender reports to all the three credit bureaus and the former should preferably be a bank or a credit union. The other factors that you need to look out for are fees and you should not go in for more $100 as initial fees. This will make you incur a high interest rate and annual fees too. A change card is one that is like a credit card however you do not need to carry a balance on them. They require you to pay your bills completely at the end of the month and they provided by Diner's Club and American Express. These cards generally do not have any kind of spending limits. This way you can build credit on credit card.

There are certain things that you need to take into account when you are taking a loan and it is wise and prudent for you to know more on the types of loans that are offered. A secured loan is one that can be attained by using money in a present account or involves the ownership of property like a car as collateral. You should consider taking the secured loan from the credit union over a bank as the former does not take your credit score into account. If you are having difficulties to acquire a loan from them you should try to get another person with a positive credit score to guarantee for you.

There is also a peer-to-peer loan that is offered by an individual investor and you can avail them from a lending site. Here you will find that investors bid on the loan and they compete on giving you the lowest interest rates. You should ensure that these sites report to all three credit bureaus and like the above if you have issues getting this type of loan you can get another person with a high credit score to vouch for you.

If you are a student you can get a federal student loan however you will not be benefitted by it once you start paying it. If you are going in for a loan from a person that you trust you should request them to co-sign so that the credit that you take is linked with theirs. This should only be done when you know and trust the person well and know that he/she will diligently pay off the loan on time. You have to be cautious in this regard as if there is any irresponsibility on their part your credit score will suffer adversely.

A GUIDE TO YOUR CREDIT RATING

Your Credit Score's Contents

Your credit score holds your personal information, such as your Social Security Number, your birth date, and your current employer. It also holds all the credit-based accounts you have opened and when you opened them. It also tells whether or not the account was paid off and how many late payments you have made.

The Components of a FICO Score

35% of your score is your payment history. This percentage of your credit score determines weather you make your payments on time.

30% of your score are the amounts of money you owe at the time. This could include credit cards, car loans, mortgages, personal loans, and other loans you may have.

15% of your score is derived from the length of your credit history. This percentage of the credit score determines how long it has been since you started purchasing on credit.

10% of your credit score is additional credit that's pending. This may be new loans or new credit cards you have just applied for.

10% of your score are the variety of credits you have with different people and companies. Though this percentage exists, it doesn't necessarily mean you have to have many types of credit to be accepted for a credit card, a loan or anything else. This percentage only truly becomes important when there is not enough information revealed about the other factors.

How third parties can use your credit report

The people and institutions you do business with; Lenders, renters, real estate agents, or any company you decide to make a purchase from all have access to your credit report. Some institutions also check your credit report once you have already obtained a loan, for example, to make sure you still meet their credit standards. Companies oftentimes look into new employee's credit history as part of a background check.

There are many laws that prohibit discrimination due to findings on your credit report such as age, gender and race. Certain laws make it illegal for creditors to refuse or disqualify credit based on discrimination. There are other laws that also protect you from similar creditor wrongdoings.

Improving Your Credit Score

One sure way to increase and better your credit score is by paying your bills on time.

Creditors look at that more than anything to determine whether they should give you credit or not. Credit history covers the past 7 years, but you have to constantly make payments on time to keep your credit score from getting lower. Bankruptcy stays in your credit report for 10 years.

There are a lot of companies out there claiming to fix your credit report in an instant. Be careful because many of these companies are scams and don't have your best interest at heart. The best way is to clean up your credit report yourself. Be honest with the people you do business with and work out payment plans so you won't delay on a due payment.

Lack of Credit History

If you are too young to have substantial credit history or you just never made any major purchases or committed to any loans, this might be reflected in your credit history. One way to make sure you have some credit history is by asking the credit reporting companies to add credit accounts that may not typically be included such as department credit cards or gas cards. Some companies charge for this service.

Credit Counseling

There are credit counselors who can find you ways to improve your credit and finally pay off your debts. They can advice you on how to approach your creditors to propose a more manageable payment plan. They can also help you establish a structured budget and show you how you can stick with it.

Credit Level

Credit Card companies determine whether they will accept your application for certain credit cards. There are 4 categories you might fall under:

1. **Great credit** -You have no missed or late payments or have no debt. If you do have debt, the debt is smaller than your income.

2. **Average to good credit** - You have 1 or more late payments but no missed payments.

There are certain companies that are most recommended by us for the last 2 categories:

- HSBD Bank cards
- American Express cards
- Discover cards
- Chase Bank cards
- Citi Cards
- Advanta
- Bank of America

3. **Bad credit** - You have high debt, missing and late payments and/or bankruptcy. Certain banks cater to people under this category.

4. **No Credit** - Certain credit cards cater to people in this category. This category means no credit history. It is usually young people under this category. Your income, your credit history, and your debts are an important factor for the next 3

items:

- The credit limit you qualify for.
- The card you qualify for (Gold, Platinum, Standard, etc.)

3. Depending on each card's term and conditions, some cards APR (Annual Percentage Rate) is higher depending on your credit history.

Do You Have Too Many Credit Cards? The Following Are Five Ways To Organize Your Budget.

In today's society and lifestyle, Americans are used to the latest and greatest electronic gadgets and modern luxuries. Credit cards are no exception. The typical American has between 5 to 10 credit cards. Using and keeping up payments for all these credit cards can be a daunting task and stressful situation, especially if you have other bills to pay. Even if you think you've already paid, you might sometimes be shocked when you get a late payment with your credit card bill. But if you do things right, you can pay on time by using these five simple methods that can greatly reduce headaches in the future.

Step 1: Simplify Due Dates.

When you have different due dates for different bills, it can cause financial chaos and harder to keep track of paid or unpaid bills. This is particularly true if you're traveling. To avoid overlooking a payment, make sure all of your bills are due on the same time. For example, make your payments fall about one week after you get paid every month. Several credit card companies will coordinate the due date with your other bill's due dates, making it easier for you to pay each month and keep track of your finances.

Step 2: Online Credit Card Payment

Paying Online is a quick and easy way to pay your credit card bills. While normal mail is an also an option, is it more time consuming and expensive. You can set up your internet payments by registering once online with credit card company. This will take a few minutes. After that, all you have to do is pay your credit card bills every month. Depending on how many credit cards you have, this process should only take a few minutes as well. It is also a great idea to pay all your other bills this way.

Step 3: Automatic Payments Are Sometimes the Best Choice

When opening a credit-based account, numerous companies give you the option to take your payment automatically from your bank account each month. It is a great choice to take this offer up so your balance doesn't fluctuate and the payment due every month stays the same.

Tip: When applying for a credit card, always be sure you read the fine print on the paper that you sign. Most, if not all, credit card companies make your card to higher interest rate after a particular amount of time has passed. Even if your card is getting automatically paid for each month, always be aware of any changes.

Step 4: Always Have an Online Account for Your Card

We can simply go online, look up the card's website, and sign in from there. An even easier way to do this is by staying organized. You can book mark all the websites you need to sign in at, and make a folder using the Favorite's option on your browser menu. This way, you can have an easy access to all of your cards' companies website addresses.

If you happen to be someone who forgets your username and/or password frequently, it's recommended to use **Norton Internet Security (TM)**. Using the Norton Identity Safe feature, it can easily fill in the website's login sheet with your information, with safety.

Tip: You will never find your financial accounts in any computer but your own. It's not very recommended to access your financial accounts from a public computer because this way, hackers have more of a chance to get your account information, without you even knowing.

Step 5: Automatic Reminders Are the Best Way to Go

When signing up for one of your cards' websites, it's best to take the option of receiving e-mails about when your bill has been issued, when your payment was due, or/and if your payment was late. If you don't want so much e-mail clutter, you should at least sign up for the automatic payment reminders only.

Tip: Though it would be nice to stay paperless and receive statements by e-mail only, there are some risks you would be taking. You could miss an important e-mail from the card company. Or if your computer crashes, you may loose many important e-mails. Some people like to stay with paper statement, which is completely fine if you feel more comfortable that way.

Visa Credit Card

You'll notice that reading and understanding all the terms of a Visa credit card application will make things better on the long run. There will be less or no unpleasant surprises like change of interest rate, annual fee or other type of fee that may be hidden in an offer's fine print.

Want a Credit Card and have Poor or No Credit?

If you have no or poor credit, there is a great chance you might be charged a membership fee for a credit card. If the company does charge a membership fee, it's ok. Once you pay for that fee, you probably won't be charged a membership fee for any other credit cards you want to get in the future.

Interest Rates

There are different types of interest rates. You have to be aware of annual percentage rates that apply to your particular credit card. Many credit card companies offer separate rates such as: introductory, cash, customary, default, and balance. Most of the time, your introductory rate will expire and your card will go to the usual retail APR. Make sure you thoroughly complete the application. In doing so, you increase your chances of being accepted. Otherwise, you might delay the application process or risk being denied.

5 HARMFUL CREDIT REPORT MYTHS

As the world rockets toward an all-digital economy, maintaining good credit is more important than ever. With that said, the use of credit cards has increased for everyday purchases, making them a key to participate in online shopping.

A 2015 study by the Federal Reserve Bank of San Francisco found that the share of American retail purchases made with cash dropped from 40 percent to 32 percent between 2012 and 2015. That's an astonishing eight percent change in just three years!

Given the importance of credit, it is no wonder that consumers are increasingly worried about their credit scores. Requests for credit reports from American credit reporting agencies have skyrocketed in recent years.

Here are five of the most pernicious myths, along with the facts about maintaining your good credit.

1: YOUR CREDIT SCORE IS A SINGLE NUMBER

A credit report does provide a single number to potential lenders, but it contains a great deal of additional information as well. Your credit report includes details about the loans you have taken out and the credit cards you have been issued. Details about your payment history are included. The report contains a wealth of information for the lender. Lenders count on all of that information when making a determination about whether to extend credit, what your credit limit will be, as well as the types of credit you might be eligible for. .

That's just for generic scores. You're also likely to have a different score calculated according to the specific criteria of lenders in real estate, for instance, and/or auto loans, and department store credit cards. the following

- **Current accounts**. Note that credit cards and mortgages are analyzed according to different criteria.
- **Payment history**. Lenders want to know whether you pay your bills on time.
- **Outstanding credit**. Reporting agencies calculate your outstanding balance compared to your total amount of available credit.
- **New credit**. If you have recently opened a bunch of new accounts, that could be a red flag.
- **Credit history**. Lenders want to know how long you have been borrowing.

Thus, lenders take much more into account than a single number.

2: CHECKING YOUR CREDIT REPORT WILL HURT YOUR SCORE

This pestilent myth has a basis in fact. If your credit report shows a great many inquiries from potential lenders, that may indicate you are in financial trouble and shopping around for loans. A flurry of requests for credit reports can be a red flag.

The credit reports you request don't show up as negatives on your history. In fact, many lenders believe it is a positive sign that consumers stay on top of their indebtedness by checking their credit histories at least once a year. It's part of good credit management. Requesting a credit report is more likely to increase than diminish your chances of getting new credit approved.

3: THE BEST WAY TO IMPROVE YOUR CREDIT SCORE IS TO PAY OFF ALL YOUR ACCOUNTS AND CLOSE THEM

This myth is partially correct.

Conversely, closing your accounts can have the opposite effect. Lenders and reporting agencies care about how much of your current credit limit you are currently using. That is, they are less interested in how much you owe than in how much you owe compared to how much you are approved to borrow. Sounds complicated, right? Think of it as a ratio. The following example will help shed more light.

If you owe $5,000 in credit card debt, that may not be significant if your credit limit across several cards is $30,000. On the other hand, if you have just one card with a limit of $5,000, then the $5,000 in current debt is quite significant and may disqualify you from opening an account with a second lender.

When you pay off your credit cards, you are decreasing the ratio of credit used to approved credit. That's great. When you close the accounts, your approved credit is reduced, and that means future credit purchases will represent a higher utilization of your total approved credit. In other words, closing the accounts actually hurts your credit score.

4: A BAD PAYMENT HISTORY DOESN'T AFFECT CREDIT SCORES ONCE ACCOUNTS ARE UP TO DATE

Unfortunately, getting caught up on payments doesn't erase your history of late payments, accounts referred to collections, and bankruptcies. All of that information stays on your report for up to seven years - or longer, depending on the type of bankruptcy.

Getting current is still important. It's a great sign and it reassures lenders that you are serious about paying your debts. Lenders understand that sometimes circumstances cause us to fall behind on payments. What they need to see is that you are committed to repay what you borrow and that you don't walk away from debt.

Missed payments stay on your credit report for three years. If you are a good customer but you are temporarily having trouble paying your bills, it's worth calling the lender to see if you can reschedule payments. Many lenders are willing to work with customers to allow a few months without payments as long as they are arranged in advance. These arrangements are not reported to credit agencies and do not harm your credit score.

But it is still true that a bad payment history continues to affect your credit score for years, even after you have brought the accounts current.

5: ALL CREDIT REPAIR SERVICES ARE SCAMS

Corrupt companies have given the credit repair industry a bad name. A simple Google search will reveal many companies that promise to erase derogatory information in your credit report for a fee.

THE HISTORY OF CREDIT AND YOUR CREDIT REPORT HISTORY

Should you repair your credit? I'm asked that more than you think. When I ask my clients, you would think the answer would be resoundingly obvious; however, as we'll see, there isn't anything obvious about it. First, let's start by reviewing what credit is, the different types of credit and how credit became such a necessary component in our society.

The word credit is derived from the Latin credo, common translation, "I believe". Credit can occur on a transactional or revolving basis and is consummated when one party provides resources to another party. What truly makes it credit, is when the party extending the resources does not expect to be immediately reimbursed, thereby creating a debt for the borrowing party. Although the concept is fairly straight forward, the problem still exists, how do you choose the people you will extend credit to and how much will you extend? We'll get into that a bit later in the article. For now, let's look at the types of loans that are readily available to those who qualify.

The Installment Loan

Let's take a trip back to New York City, circa 1807, Cowperthwaite & Sons Furniture Store began an installment credit plan allowing people to buy today but pay over a period of time. To start, a down payment was made by the customer that was followed by monthly payments of equal amounts. The concept mirrors the "non-credit" card loan payments we make today. Cowperthwaite & Sons Furniture Store was extremely discriminant as too the customers they would allow to purchase furniture on their installment plan. They hand-picked their credit customers to keep those who defaulted to a minimum.

Fast forward almost 50 years to 1850 and the cutting edge of technology, the Singer Peddle Sewing Machine. The sewing machine, at the time, presented a unique challenge; being sold for $100 how was Isaac Singer going to mass produce and mass distribute the sewing machine. Edward Clark, co-founder of the Singer Sewing Machine Company, originated the "hire-purchase plan", the prototype for all installment selling or time payment purchases. As a result, people who would not be able to afford a sewing machine under normal circumstances could now purchase a Singer sewing machine and pay later. Even better, they could increase their productivity, earn more money and improve their position in life.

Revolving Credit

First introduced by the Strawbridge and Clothier Department Store (also Hecht's and Macy's in future years) in the 1960's, the revolving line of credit gave people the opportunity to buy things without paying for them that day and it also gave the store another stream of revenue in interest. In revolving lines of credit, the terms aren't fixed as they are in the installment loan model. Soon after the department stores began capitalizing on the "charge cards", banks jumped into the mix with larger limit credit cards, after all, loaning money is their business.

Here is an example of how a revolving credit actually works. You apply for a revolving line of credit, a credit card, and you are approved to spend up to $500. You immediately go out and purchase a new bike for $75. You can now only spend a maximum of $425 before reaching your credit limit. Now, you purchase a concert ticket for $75, leaving $350 as your available credit limit. At the end of the month, you have a decision, pay off your current debt, $150 or, don't pay the debt this month. By not paying the debt, you will have to pay interest on the $150 and you limit remains $350 until the debt is paid. Revolving credit, especially credit cards, typically have high interest rates and it's not uncommon to see interest rates exceeding 15%.

As you can see, revolving credit provides a unique and valuable service - when used responsibly. In this example above, you used your revolving line of credit as needed, if you had obtained an Installment loan of $500 you would have had to pay interest on the full amount, $500, rather than just the amount that you had used, $150. Once you pay the $150 - plus interest back, your available limit will then increase back to its previous maximum,

$500. When used irresponsibly, revolving credit can become an unmanageable nightmare. So, the questions remains, when to approve and how much.

The Big Three and Two More

Does anyone remember the "Welcome Wagon" representatives? You move into a new neighborhood and the Welcome Wagon representative sets a time to come over and deliver baked goods, coupons, advertisements for local businesses, etc. Well that's not all they were doing. Retailer's Credit, now Equifax, used to gather data about you during those "welcome visits". Information such as, race, ethnicity, the quality of your home, furnishings, their opinion of your character, etc. Back then, trying to see what was in you report was nearly impossible. It could be riddled with mistakes, error and incorrect information but you would never know. Even if you did know, there was nothing you could do.

Today, there are three mainstream Consumer **credit Reporting Agencies** (CRA), Equifax, Experian and TransUnion. The fourth, Innovis, is similar in nature to the main CRAs; however, Innovis is not used nearly as much in terms of reporting. Companies who use them will usually say, we report to all four bureaus.

There is a fifth bureau out there called **PRBC**, it is similar to the other four CRAs in that it is an FCRA (**Fair Credit Reporting Act)** compliant national data repository. However, PRBC differs in a few distinct and consumer favorable ways. Consumers are able to self-enroll and report their own non-debt payment history.

They can build a positive credit file based on alternative data, such as rent, utilities, cable, telephone, and insurance that are not automatically or traditionally reported to the other bureaus.

Under the FCRA credit bureaus are legally known in the United States as Consumer Reporting Agencies. There are a number of important consumer protections which are made available as a remedy to consumers by the following acts and/or regulations, they are as follows; FCRA, **Fair & Accurate Credit Transaction Act** (FACTA), **Fair Credit Billing Act** (FCBA) and Regulation B. Additionally, there are two government agencies responsible for overseeing credit bureaus and the data furnishers which supply them with their data. The **Federal Trade Commission** (FTC) is responsible for overseeing all consumer credit bureaus. Data furnishers are regulated by the **Office of the Comptroller of the Currency** (OCC).

So now that we have the landscape of the industry, let's dig in a little and see how your credit affects just you. To start, take a snapshot in your mind of how you pay bills and accumulate debt. Would you say you're responsible, irresponsible or somewhere in the middle. Just having that idea, , you probably have some idea of what is being report by the CRAs about your credit. Now just so we're on the same page here, all of these reporting agencies have different information based on what companies (the furnishers or creditors) report to them. Hardly an exact science and sometimes I wonder how fair our system actually is, but it's our chosen system so let's move on.

Based on the data available on your credit reports, you are assigned a number between 300, the worst and 850, or perfect. The data that is looked at can range from being late with a payment, having a charge-off to public records, such as, bankruptcies as well as liens or judgments. The most recognized and widely used credit score is the FICO Score, a credit score developed by the Fair Isaac Corporation. Lenders use your FICO score and other like it to help them make billions of educated credit decisions every year. Fair Isaac calculates the FICO Score based solely on information in consumer credit reports maintained at the credit reporting agencies. Ultimately, the FICO score estimates your level of future credit risk - remember, future prediction are best evaluated on past performance. Meaning **if you did it before, we assume you will do it again**.

CBS News reported four out of every five credit reports contains some error or inaccurate information, that's eighty percent! Where could you find a job where you could be wrong 80% of the time? How about a school you could be right only 20% of the time? That job and that school don't exist but the credit bureaus, seemingly the largest oligopoly of our time, are satisfied with those statistics and defend the industry to any naysayers the first chance it gets. How does this affect your report? Let's take a look.

Your Credit Report

Everyone in the United States over the age of eighteen is a consumer, from a technical perspective anyway. You can be issued credit by banks, car dealerships, department stores, gas stations, you name it. It's usually your start to becoming an adult, the next phase of your life after high school. Let's say when you started high school as **a little freshman**, some senior walked the halls spewing negative information about you, saying you're smelly and have a contagious rash. Now you have to start making friends that will follow you for the next four years. Not an easy task after the jerk senior went around spreading that inaccurate information.

So let's break this down. **Jerk senior**, or the Consumer credit Reporting Agency, has bad or erroneous information, or credit data, about you and wrongfully spreads it through the school, or the credit community, hurting your otherwise immaculate reputation, or credit report. Hopefully you are catching on.

Now, the senior has to answer to **the school principal**, or the Federal Trade Commission, who oversees the rules of the school. The senior rats out another student, the creditor or furnisher, thereby admitting the data he had was second hand and could not be verified. The principal ensures the senior is set straight and sends him on his way with accurate information about the freshman. Once he has this data, he and the freshman become best of friends. So in our example, what if the student wasn't smelly but did have a rash he was trying to get rid of. Well if the rash isn't verifiable and is in a place that can't be seen - it can't be used against him now, can it?. Same with your credit. Your report can say whatever they want it to say; however, by law, at any time you request, the CRA must verify the data it reports. Data such as, contracts, late checks, agreements, public record, etc.

What we have just learned is your credit report is basically your consumer reputation. Walk into a furniture store and fill out a credit app, will you get approved or turned down. What if the salesperson is your neighbor, hopefully you get approved. Otherwise, there will be a certain level of embarrassment for sure. Why chance it? You don't play around with your personal reputation why play around with your consumer reputation?

Now you can certainly go it alone with the CRAs, creditors, furnishers, collections agencies, etc. and the federal government requires any credit repair organization to tell you that. We don't have special relationships or powers to do anything you can't do yourself, other than experience and education in the industry. To that, I always ask, if you were being charged with a serious crime and the judge looked at the attorney and made him tell you he doesn't have special relationships or powers to do anything you can't do yourself, other than experience and education in the industry. **Would that make you want to represent yourself**? Remember two things they say about self-representation in court, **"a lawyer who acts for him or herself has a fool for a client"** and **"ignorance is not a valid defense"**.

However, when selecting a credit report organization, I do caution you to use due diligence and/or red flags of illicit or illegal behavior. Here are some key things to look out for:

- **Avoid** Credit Repair Services That Promise the Impossible

- **Avoid** Credit Repair Services That Suggest You Create a New Identity

- **Select** Credit Repair Services with Credible References

- **Avoid** Credit Repair Services Requesting any Payment Upfront (It's illegal and against federal law.)

- **Avoid** Credit Repair Services Who Avoid Using a Mutual Contract.

TERMINOLOGY YOU NEED TO KNOW TO UNDERSTAND YOUR CREDIT REPORT

NEGATIVE CREDIT CAN COME WITH SERIOUS PROBLEMS

Your credit report is aexact picture of your "consumer character" and as such, can have some pretty bad implications with the wrong information. Our lives for the most part revolve around the decisions we make and we are presented with those decisions daily, sometimes multiple times a day. Poor decisions, such as overspending or over extending yourself from a credit perspective can have a lasting effect on you and your ability to continue making similar decisions at a later date and time, sometimes, in the case of a bankruptcy, up to ten years. So to an extent, your credit report is direct reflection of the consumer freedom you will enjoy or with negative credit, it will be a direct reflection of your lack of freedom.

Negative credit can affect you in many ways, from getting housing, a car loan, a job, and even security clearance. If you have been turned down for a mortgage, a car loan, an apartment, or a job because of your credit, you know from personal experience how a negative credit report can painfully impact your life. Unfortunately, there isn't anything that can solve these problems quickly. However, there is a specific process and laws in effect that can help you to start fixing your credit. There are two ways to do this:

1) hire someone to do it for you, or

2) do it yourself and spend the time necessary figuring it out and preparing the necessary documents. When doing it yourself, you may want to seek the guidance of a professional to be sure you did it correctly.

THE GOOD, THE BAD AND THE UGLY

Let's take a look at what's good and what's bad. First, let's set the parameters to which we are evaluated. The FICO system, a system that summarizes your credit risk for lenders, produces a score between 300 and 850 and we all fall somewhere in that range. The interest rate you get when you apply for a loan will depend on this score and that can be worth thousands over the life of a loan.

Scenario 1, if you do not have any negative marks against your credit, and by negative we are referring to collections activity, late payments, tax liens, judgments, etc. in the last 24 months and no bankruptcy or foreclosure in the last five years with a credit score above 700, you have a good credit profile.

Scenario 2, if your credit score is below 630 and you have all or even some of the items mentioned above, you have a bad or less than favorable credit profile.

Scenario 3, if your score falls somewhere in the middle of the scores above and you have some of the items mentioned above, you have a mediocre credit profile.

In the credit scoring business, different scoring companies use different scoring models. They do this because credit isn't just credit - there are mortgages, consumer credit, and revolving credit and installment loans. Scores will and should vary between the different scoring methods depending on the facts.

HOW TO READ YOUR CREDITREPORT

Your credit report contains a wealth of information about your financial activity. Although credit reports are not easiest reports to understand, the bureaus providing the reports have tried to make them as user-friendly as possible.

Personal Information

The first section of your report will cover basic information like your name, address, and place(s) of employment. This section is used to identify you as the reports owner. Most likely, previous addresses and places of employment will also be included.

In this section, it's not uncommon to have misspellings of your name or variations thereof. Because these misspellings and variations usually link you to a piece of credit, credit reporting agencies will usually leave these variations. **It's your job to** ensure your personal information is identifying you and not someone else.

Account History

This section of your credit report contains the majority of the information about your credit. This section lists each of your accounts and details how you paid on each of them. Your account history will be extremely detailed and will most likely be the hardest section to read; however, **it's important you read through all of it to make sure the information is being reported accurately**.

As far as collection accounts, they may appear as part of the account history or in a separate section, usually labeled negative credit. Where it appears will depend on the company providing your credit report. Within the account history, there will be several pieces of sub-information.

Company name of the institution reporting the information .

- **Account number** associated with the account. The account number may be scrambled or shortened for privacy purposes.
- **Type of account**, i.e. revolving account, education loan, auto loan.
- **Terms of repayment**. Installment loans include the number of payments. Revolving accounts may leave this section blank or as "revolving".

- **Date opened.** The month and year the account was established.
- **High credit** is the highest amount ever charged on the credit card. For installment loans, high credit is the original loan amount.
- **Credit limit** or loan amount.
- **Balance.** The amount owed on the account at the time data was reported.
- **Past Due.** Amount past due at the time the data was reported.
- **Account status.** Indicates the status of the account, i.e. current, past due, charge-off. Even if your account is current, it might contain information about previous delinquencies.
- **Payment history.** Indicates your monthly payment status since the time your account was established.
- **Date reported.** The last time the data was updated by the creditor.

Public Records

This section will include information like bankruptcies, judgments, tax liens, state and country court records, and, in some states, overdue child support. Depending on the type of account, a public record may remain on your credit report between seven and ten years, ten years being reserved for bankruptcies. This section is a collection of the bigger mistakes, not criminal arrests or convictions but enough to severely damage your credit.

Credit Inquiries

This section provides a detailed list all parties who have accessed your credit report within the past two years. While your version of the credit report lists several credit inquiries, not all of these appear on the lenders' and creditors' versions. Only **"hard" inquiries** are shown to lenders. These are inquiries made when a lender checks your credit report to approve your credit application. Your version will also include **"soft" inquiries** consisting of inquiries made by lenders for promotional purposes.

Initially, if you need help, try your loan officer if you are applying for credit and see if they will take some time to explain it to you. Most of them will try to help as best they can, especially if you are trying to repair your credit because the loan officer would eventually benefit when he originates a loan for you. If you were not working with a loan officer and you are trying the DIY credit repair method, you might consider a free consultation with a credit repair company to learn the basics. They will assist you in understanding your credit report and should tell you some of the advantages and disadvantages of doing credit repair on your own or through a credit repair company.

HOW TO AVOID MISTAKES ON YOUR CREDIT REPORT

We have developed eight effective strategies for preventing mistakes on your credit report. We wish you much success.

1) Beware Of Debts & Credit You Don't Use

Just as it is very easy to apply for a store credit card, it is also easy to forget you have it. It is important to remember that the account will remain on your report and affect your score as long as it is open. Don't make the mistake of having credit lines and cards you don't need. It makes you look more risky from a lenders point of view.

Also, having many accounts you don't use increases the odds that you will forget about an old account and stop making payments on it, resulting in a lowered credit score. **Keep only the accounts you use regularly and consider closing your other accounts**. Having fewer accounts will make it easier for you to keep track of your debts and will increase the chances of you having a good credit score.

However, realize that when you close an account, the record of the closed account remains on your credit report and can affect your credit score for some time. In fact, closing unused credit accounts may actually **cause your credit score to drop in the short-term**, as you will have higher credit balances spread out over a smaller overall credit account base.

For example, if your unused credit limits amount to $2,000, and your regularly used accounts also have a credit limit of $2,000, you have $4,000 of available credit. If you close your unused accounts and owe $1,000 on the accounts you use regularly, you have gone from using one-fourth of your credit ($1,000 owed on a possible $4,000) to using one-half of your credit ($1,000 from a possible $2,000). This will actually cause your credit risk rating to drop. **In the long term**, though, not having extra temptation to charge, and not having credit you don't need, **will help your budget**.

2) Avoid Having Many Credit Report Inquiries

An inquiry is noted every time someone looks at your credit report. Don't make the mistake of allowing too many inquiries on your credit report, as it may appear that you have been rejected by multiple lenders. This means that you should be careful about who looks at it. If you are shopping for a loan (finding the lowest interest rate based on your credit), shop around within a short period of time, as inquiries made within a few days of each other will generally be lumped together and counted as one inquiry.

You can also cut down the number of inquiries on your account by approaching lenders you have already researched and are interested in doing business with. By researching first, and approaching second, you will likely have only a few lenders accessing your credit report at the same time, which can help save your credit score.

3) Don't Mistakenly Over-Use Online Loan Rate Comparisons

Online loan rate quotes are easy to obtain. Just type in some personal information and within seconds you can receive a quote on your car loan, personal loan, student loan, or mortgage. This is free and convenient, leading many people to compare several companies at once in order to get the best possible loan rate. The problem is that since online quotes are a fairly recent phenomenon, credit bureaus **count each quote as an inquiry.** This means that if you compare too many companies online, your credit score will suffer.

This does not mean you shouldn't seek online quotes for loan. In fact, online loan quotes are a great resource that can help you get the very best rates on your next loan. It just means that you should **carefully research** companies and narrow down your choices to only a few lenders before making inquiries. This will help ensure that the number of inquires on your credit report is small, and your score will remain strong.

4) Don't Make The Mistake Of Thinking You Only Have One Credit Report

Most people mistakenly speak of having a "credit score" when in fact credit reports often include three or more credit scores. There are three major credit bureaus in the United States that develop credit reports and calculate credit scores, as well as a number of smaller credit bureau companies. In addition, some larger lenders calculate their own credit risk score based on information in your credit report. When improving your credit report, **you should not focus on one number only**. You should contact the three major credit bureaus and work on improving all three credit scores.

5) Don't Close Multiple Credit Accounts

Many people make the mistake of closing multiple credit accounts in an effort to improve their credit score. If you close an account you need (for example, if you close all your credit card accounts), then you may find yourself in the position where **you need to reapply for credit**. Not only is this inconvenient, but the inquiries from credit companies can actually hurt your credit report. Additionally, credit bureaus will actually look favorably upon your credit report if they can see that you have a **(good) long-term credit history**. For example, don't make the mistake of closing a credit card account you have had for the past 10 years, as this may actually hurt your credit report.

If you have credit accounts that you don't use, or if you have too many credit lines, then by all means pay off some and close them.

Doing so may help your credit score, as long as you don't close **long-term accounts** you need. In general, **close your newest accounts first**, and only when you are certain you will not need that credit in the near future.

Closing your accounts is a bad idea if:

A) **You will be applying for a loan soon.** The closing of your accounts will make your score drop in the short-term and will not allow you to qualify for good loan rates.

B **Your debt to credit ratio increases**). For example, you owe $10,000 now and have access to an extra $5,000. However, after closing some accounts you are only left with $1,000. This brings you closer to maxing out your credit and in turn hurts your report.

6) Don't Assume Only One Action Will Improve Your Credit Report

An example of a common mistake that some debtors make is believing that paying off a credit card bill will boost their score by 50 points, while closing an unused credit account will result in 20 more points. **Improving your credit report is certainly not this simple.** How much any one action will affect your credit score is impossible to gauge. It will depend on multiple factors, including your current credit score, and which credit bureau is calculating it. In general, the higher your credit score, the more small factors - such as one unpaid bill - will affect you. When repairing the score on your credit report, you should not equate specific credit repair actions with numbers. The idea is to do as many things as you can to improve your credit report.

7) Having No Loans & No Debt Will Not Improve Your Credit Report

Some people make the mistake of believing that owing no money, having no credit cards, and avoiding the whole world of credit will help improve the score on their credit report. **In reality, the opposite is true.** Lenders want to know about your past ability to handle credit, and the only way they can tell is by the score on your credit report. Having no credit at all can actually be worse for your credit score than having a few credit accounts that you pay off on time. If you currently have no credit accounts at all, **opening a low balance credit card can actually boost your credit score.**

Think of your credit report like a **basketball game**. The player who **scores many points** in every game is considered to be a great player, and will receive higher financial rewards than those who **only score a few points**. Those who **don't even play** basketball have no scores to "report" to the game officials. In the world of credit reports, the debtor who scores the most points is someone who pays off their credit accounts every month. They will receive financial rewards through easier access to loans and lower interest rates, while those who have no credit accounts have a very low credit score.

8) Never Do Anything Illegal To Repair Your Credit Report

It seems pretty obvious, but plenty of people make the mistake of lying about their credit score or even falsifying their loan applications because they are ashamed of a bad score. Not only is this illegal, but it is also completely ineffective at repairing your credit report. Your credit score is easy to check and, not only will you not fool lenders by lying on your credit report, but you may actually face legal action as a result of your dishonesty.

HOW TO FIX A NEGATIVE CREDIT REPORT IN JUST 3 SIMPLE STEPS

If you want to get rid of negative credit you can easily take a few steps to completely turn it around and see a significant improvement in your credit score. Thousands of people face the same problems and assume it takes a credit professional or credit repair service to do it for them. These offline and online credit services don't come cheap and often people spend their hard-earned money trying to fix negative or bad credit.

First of all you may not know what is actually on your credit report today. You may assume you have bad credit based on your payment history in the past or you haven't had the courage to get a copy of your credit report even though it's free. Many resist this because of the fear of what they think they may find . However you may be surprised. There may be entries on your credit report that are totally false and can be easily corrected or there may be entries you can easily change with a little documentation.

Really it's not that difficult to get these corrections taken care of on your credit report. You can actually take care of it pretty fast and it won't cost you a dime other than a first class stamp. You can do a better job than any credit repair clinic because you're in the position to actually add some positive credit marks to your report if you know how to do it and I'll explain below.

Okay these are the 3 simple steps to repair your credit history.

1. First get a copy of your **free credit report** if you don't already have a CURRENT copy. Everyone is entitled to a free credit report every year according to federal government laws. You can get an absolutely free annual credit report online instantly at the approved Web site **annualcreditreport.com**. You'll be able to print it out as soon as you provide identification.

You can also call **1-877-322-8228**. When you call you'll get an automated service. Know what phone number you're going to use as that is a requirement in the process. However it will take about 15 days to get the report. You can also write but instant online or calling is easiest. This free service is sponsored by the three credit reporting agencies - Equifax, Experian and TransUnion.

Now you must know that you won't get your credit rating or score when you get the report. There is an additional charge to get a score. However if you recently applied for credit and were turned down, **call the lender and ask what your score is**. You can usually find out that way for free.

Once you have your credit report in hand, sit down and note any negative items or anything that doesn't seem right to you. You may find a few mistakes, sometimes even with your birth date or other personal information. These are easily corrected. There can be some totally false information such as credit information for someone else with the same name or similar name.

2. **Write a dispute letter**. It's easy to write a dispute letter. If you're not sure how to do this, sit down and pretend you're writing a letter to a friend. It does not have to be fancy and it can be in your own handwriting if legible or typed out. Don't make it too hard. Make a list of the bad credit marks or wrong information that you want to dispute. Make sure to keep it as short as possible and don't add any fluff. Get the facts as you know them. If you have any documentation to include to **'back you up'** then add this or include copies with your dispute letter.

When the credit bureau gets your letter they will do an investigation and will either verify the item in question and remove or fix it - or they will be unable to verify the negative credit information to remove it.

If they notify you that they are unable to verify any negative credit mark thus not removing it, then you can still dispute it by sending another letter asking how they arrived at their decision. This is called a **'method of verification'** or sometimes **'procedural request'**. If the dispute is regarding a creditor the credit reporting bureau and the creditor must both provide you with adequate proof of their decision. Otherwise they are required by law to remove the negative credit mark from your credit history.

3. How to **get positive credit marks** on your credit report. This is simple to do over a period of a few months to start building a positive credit history. Get department store and/or gas credit cards and use them. Pay them off on time. Make note that these

usually come with higher interest rates so compare rates first. Pay a little more than you owe and pay a little early. Paying online ensures that your payment arrives and is not lost in the mail.

Keep a bill calendar and write on it when payments are due and another notation on the calendar a few days before so that you make the payment online early. If you wait till the last minute, the Web site may be down for maintenance or their may be other network issues. But in any event make sure to make the payment before it's due. Try to get an installment type of loan or automobile loan through your bank or credit union.

Be aware that if you try to buy a car or other vehicle that the car dealer will contact several lenders to get the best interest rate and EACH one of these will contribute a mark to your credit report. This can affect your credit score, also called FICO. So try to get a **pre-approved loan** before you head to an auto dealer. If you can do this over a few months you will build up a recent and good credit history fast. No credit repair service will be able to build up this positive history for you.

CREDIT RATING! WHAT DO YOU KNOW ABOUT IT?

There could be so much confusion when it comes to the terms such as credit rating, credit history or credit status. The goal of this is to give you more insight into the meaning of all these terminologies and how they affect you as a prospective borrower.

Let's start with the question of what is credit rating or credit scoring? This is an independent or individual statistical evaluation of one's ability to repay a loan or debt based on your previous borrowing and repayment history.

Two things to note here: firstly, the word independent or individual, which means that one's assessment of credit worthiness, varies from one lender to another, so basically each company has its own criteria to decide whether it will lend you money or not and how much risk they are willing to take. The other thing to note is "Previous borrowing and repayment history", this is what is termed your Credit history - it is part of the information held about you by Credit Reference Agencies detailing how good or bad you have handled credit in the past.

What information do credit agencies hold about me?

Some of the information which credit reference agencies hold about an individual includes:

- Name and Date of Birth
- The Electoral Register
- County Court Judgments
- Credit Payment History
- Bankruptcy & Administration orders
- House repossession... e.t.c

The most important of this data is your credit/repayment history which states your credit accounts, the account opening date, loan amount and how often you make payments. The information about your credit account is held in your record for about six year after the account has been settled. It will also be good to make mention of some information the credit agencies don't know about you such as: Criminal records, Fines, Savings Account, information about family members, Student Loans e.t.c.

So, What is My credit Rating?

That is the question most people will love to find a straight answer to, thinking probably that there is a list somewhere showing people's name and their credit ratings, really there is no such list available, not anywhere in the whole world, neither is there any blacklist of all people with bad credit rating. The process is simple, lenders use information from credit reference agencies to assess how well you have handled credit in the past (This is known as **Credit Check**), each lender analyses the information according to its own rules, and so you may be turned down by one company but accepted by another. However if you have not handled credit properly in the past, this will show in your credit report file held at the credit reference agencies and may reduce your chance of getting loan from lenders when they consult the agencies.

What Actions affect how a prospective lender may rate me?

- Bad credit history
- Prolonged borrowing with late repayments
- Unemployment
- Series of credit line
- Bankruptcy
- Outstanding debt
- Inaccurate information held by credit reference agencies
- No history of borrowing
- Not meeting up with a particular lender's specific requirements
- Details not on voters register
- Frauds or identity thefts

Some of these actions may not be directly under the control of the borrower; while actions such as late payments can be avoided; inaccurate data held by credit agencies is totally out of the control of the borrower, what about if the borrower identity has been stolen and used for some fraudulent activities? This calls for a real need for everyone to check their files regularly. Even if you have not been refused credit, it is always advisable to check your files at least once a year for up-to-date and correct information.

How to check your credit history

Under the Consumer Credit Act 1974 you have a statutory right to see what information credit reference agencies hold about you. Credit Reference Agencies can provide you with a statutory credit report for a fee of about $2 this contains just your basic credit file. However with a slightly higher fee, most of these agencies can provide you with an instant online access to more detailed information about your credit status with an ongoing credit monitoring service. For more information, you can check out these credit reference agencies:

- Experian
- Equifax
- Call Credit

Does bad credit history mean i can never get credit?

Although this is an important factor which is placed so much emphasis upon when it comes to getting out credit or loans from high street banks and major financial institutions, this might mean a very poor chance of one getting out a loan with such companies especially if you have big projects to carry out such as business loans or mortgages. However, if you need credit on a smaller scale, you may stand a 100% chance with companies such as the home credit providers.

CREDIT RATINGS

How banks decide who to lend to:

A bank will basically use three different types of information when deciding whether to give you a loan, credit card or mortgage. Firstly, it will look at the **information on your application form**. As well as items such as your age, income and marital status, it will look at how often you've moved jobs or home. This will give it an idea of how 'stable' you are financially.

Secondly, it will look at how you've acted **when it's dealt with you in the past**, so how you've operated your current account and whether you've repaid loans on time. Obviously, if you've never dealt with the company before this stage will be skipped.

The last of the three steps is to look at **your credit report**. Having looked at each of these three sources of information, a lender will then assess how you measure up on various points and build up its own credit score for you. If your credit score is greater than a certain number, your application will usually be approved. If it's not, then you'll either be rejected or offer a smaller loan or one at a higher rate of interest.

Unfortunately, lenders don't disclose how they score individuals. Each company will assign a different rating to various issues, depending on their experience with customers in the past, so this is why you might be rejected for credit by one lender but accepted by another. Although it's a popular misconception, there is no such thing as a **'credit blacklist'**.

What kind of public records your credit report contains ?

Credit reports contain many different types of information about you. For example they contain matters of public record such as whether you are on the **Electoral Roll** (a prerequisite for approval by most lenders).

Your credit report will also show whether you've had any **County Court Judgments** (CCJ) against you or whether you've been made bankrupt, are in an **Individual Voluntary Arrangement** (IVA) or a debt management programme.

Any recent applications for credit you've made are also shown on your credit report. Usually this information is kept for twelve months but Callcredit keeps it for two years. Whether the application was accepted or not and the amount is not recorded but obviously a lender will able to see if you then went on to have a loan with the company concerned.

Several applications for credit in quick succession can affect your chances of getting further credit as a lender may assume you have been refused or are in danger of taking on too much debt. One way around this problem is to ask for quote for credit rather than making a formal application. This won't appear on your credit report and you'll need to make a formal application if you do then proceed to take out a loan. You can also ask for a quotation search rather than an application search to be made.

This will appear on your credit report but any lender will be able to see it wasn't a formal application.

If you have any financial associations with another person a note of this will appear on your credit report. In this instance, a financial association means having, for example, a joint loan, bank account, credit card or mortgage. A financial association allows a lender to access the other person's credit report when assessing whether you're suitable to lend to.

Just because you're married to or living with someone, their credit history won't automatically be associated with yours. Additionally, any credit problems previous residents or tenants of your property have had won't affect your ability to get credit.

Finally, any debt agreements you have or that have been settled within in the last six years will also be recorded on your credit report, together with a summary of your recent payment record where applicable. If you are in arrears or in default then this will be shown. Not all lenders supply information to all the credit report companies so it may be that not all your debts will appear. Some lenders only supply negative information so a record might only appear if you've been in arrears or default.

As well as debt agreements, mobile and pay TV payment information may appear on your credit report. Information relating to the payment on utility bills or council tax does not however. Rather perversely, a lack of credit in the past can mean it's more difficult to get accepted for a loan. Lenders prefer to see a clean credit history rather than none at all.

CREDIT FREEZE - HOW TO DO IT AND WHAT IT DOES

A credit freeze for those who aren't quite familiar yet, is a way to block your credit reports, making it difficult or impossible for others to loan or open a credit account using your name. This is because while a freeze is in place, no one will be able to open an account using your name, not even you. Insurers, lenders, and anyone who would like to access your file will not be able to unless otherwise you are able to lift the freeze. You can have the freeze lifted or thawed if you would like, but you will have to provide the bureaus with a personal identification number and a few days' notice. Most people usually resort to this method when under circumstances that would put their identity in danger for theft.

But as advantageous as this may be, you should also be aware that putting a freeze on your credit files will also delay, interfere or prohibit creditors from accessing them. This can be a bit of a problem especially during those times for when you are applying for credit. Upon placing freeze, you are provided with a personal identification number which is what you use to remove the freeze or grant access to any person or creditor for a specific period of time.

To place a freeze on your credit, you will simply need to write each credit bureau to request for one. Be sure that within this letter, you are able to include your proof of address, proof of your social security number and a photo ID. Upon receiving the letter and upon approval, the bureaus will then mail you your personal identification number.

Some of the reasons you might consider freezing your credit would be:

- You've already been a victim of a "New Account" fraud in the past.
- You found out that your personal identifying information has been compromised.
- Your wallet or purse has gone missing.
- You are unable to trust those who are close to you.
- You just need it for peace of mind.

Regardless of whatever reasons you may have, freezing your credit files can be considered as both a good and bad thing. Thankfully, the freeze can be easily lifted for when you feel that the threat has passed and placed again when you feel your account or financial well-being is in danger, making it a convenient way to safeguard your credit score from unwanted situations.

CREDIT FREEZE, FRAUD AND YOU

What is a credit freeze and what makes it different from credit fraud alert? The credit freeze was first introduced in California in 2003. Today, however, a credit freeze can be done in all 50 States and can be requested from any of the three major credit bureaus. Unlike a credit fraud alert which only lasts for up to 90 days, a credit freeze will last for as long as the owner of the report doesn't request that his report be thawed. Therefore, if you want to apply for a new credit card or you plan to get a loan, you need to notify the credit bureau in advance to get the freeze be lifted.

The Unfreezing of the credit report can take just few minutes or up to a week, depending on the State or the credit bureau issuing the report. You have the option to choose whether you want to unfreeze your credit report permanently or for just a limited time period. Also, within this period, you can limit the list of people who can look in your report.

Why Freeze your Credit

Putting your credit report on a freeze definitely gives you more protection from identity theft or fraud. Going through the procedures of freezing and unfreezing and paying a certain amount, usually about $10 each time is definitely worth spending your money on, rather than, putting yourself at risk of being victimized by ID theft or fraud.

How do you ask for a credit freeze?

A fraud alert can be done by phone but if you want to freeze your report, you need to send a letter of request to the credit bureau via registered mail. Generally, at least two proofs of residency such as a billing statement or a copy of your driver's license is required. The cost for a credit freeze ranges from $10 to $12. Unfreezing or thawing will also cost you about $10 to $12 for each bureau.

More Credit Precautions

But aside from putting your credit report on a freeze, what other steps can you do on your own? Here are valuable tips you should not overlook:

- **Shred all** receipts, past billing statements, and old documents that contain your bank information or any of your personal details on it. If you don't have shredder, tear the document into tiny bits and throw the pieces in separate trash bins.

- **Don't write** your bank information, credit card numbers, PIN codes or passwords on just any sheet of paper. Keep all these important details in one log book and keep it in a secured place or a locked storage.

- If you want to use your credit card for shopping online, ask your credit card company for a **different credit card number** that you can use exclusively for online transactions.

- **Access your online account regularly.** Most credit cards today provide an online account service where you can check the status of your account over the internet at any time. Thus, you don't have to go out of your way to visit your local bank to update yourself. It takes only five minutes at most to access your account from your computer.

- Sign up for your **credit card's fraud protection service.** Some credit cards provide this feature automatically but if your credit card doesn't, it's a good idea to sign up. This service will give a quicker response from your credit card issuer in case your wallet or your credit card gets stolen.

- If you need to **get in touch with an agent** from any of three credit bureaus- Experian, Equifax or Trans Union- by phone, visit **gethuman.com** to access the latest contact numbers where you can speak with a human representative from the credit bureaus and not just a recorded message.

IDENTITY THEFT

Have you been a victim of identity theft? Do you have concerns that someone may get your credit information without your authorization?

Identity theft is worse than anything that you will go through. Months, in some cases years of problems because someone else used your identity to obtain all kinds of things, from clothing to trips around the world. **All of this because someone, somewhere easily opened an account using your information.** There are ways of protecting yourself from identity theft... but which ones really work?

A credit freeze is one good protection against identity theft and credit fraud. Currently there are 50 states with laws that allow residents and victims of identity theft the option to freeze their credit This means if someone tries to use your information on an application to obtain credit, even if that "someone" is you, the application will be denied and no credit will be issued.

The laws concerning credit freezing vary by state. There are some states that do not have any laws allowing for credit freeze, then others that specifically require that you already be a victim of identity theft in order to have a credit freeze placed on your file and then others that allow anyone that is a resident of their state to pay a small fee to have a freeze placed on their account.

To have a credit freeze placed on your account, you must contact each credit bureau and ask what information that they will require from you in order to place a credit freeze on your account. If you are married, then you and your spouse will need to **send in separate letters** (send only certified letters). Generally, you will need to provide your full name, date of birth, social security number and residence for the past 5 years. If you qualify for a credit freeze then within a couple of weeks you will receive a PIN number from the credit bureaus.

You always have the ability **to lift the credit freeze temporarily by logging into the credit bureau websites and entering your PIN,** or you can provide your PIN to a potential lender if you are applying for credit. If this becomes too much of a hassle for you, you can request a permanent removal of the freeze.

THE 5 C'S OF CREDIT

Are you ready for the home loan process? Knowing the 5 Cs of credit will help you understand just what your lender is looking for. We'll let you take an inside peek at the training tips we give to the loan officers who come to Complete Mortgage Processing for help:

Credit Character - In analyzing a borrower's credit history, you first need to have a goal in mind. The goal should be to confirm that the borrower's history meets or exceeds the credit guidelines for the product/program you wish to have the loan underwritten to. In making the confirmation, you should consider these factors separately as not meeting any one of them could drop the borrower into a lower credit grade. Compare the credit report to the lender's underwriting matrix or underwriting guidelines to evaluate the following:

The FICO score - Is it within an acceptable range for the loan program? How does the lender determine the score -the lower of two or the middle of three?

The mortgage payment history - Is the number of late payments at or below the lender's standard?

The number and characteristic of each open trade lines:

The quantity - Are there enough traditional credit trade lines? If not, is alternative credit allowed. If so, what are the documentation requirements for alternative credit sources?

The installment/revolving account payment history - Is the number of late payments at or below that stated standard?

The installment/revolving account age or seasoning - Does the account meet the aging requirement -12 months, 24 months, etc.

The installment/revolving account credit limit - Does the account meet the required standard for credit line limit?

Here is an **example** of a lender's trade line requirements:Minimum of 3 trade lines, 1 year established, with 1 credit line of $1,000 or more

Public records - Are there any? Were they disclosed? What is the status? How will they affect the underwriting decision?

Social security number(s) - Are they consistent with the information disclosed on the 1003?

Derogatory credit - Other derogatory credit. Can we document the status? Has it been satisfied or will it be satisfied on or before closing?Inquiries -How many have there been in the past 6 months?

Duplicate entries - Can you confirm that it is in fact a duplicate? Can you get it removed prior to underwriting submission?

Capacity - Regardless of how good a borrower's credit is, they must demonstrate the financial capacity to handle the debt. Reviewing the borrower's past income and employment history is the best indicator of the ability to handle future debt. The following items should be considered when analyzing your borrower's capacity:

Stability - Has the borrower's employment remained stable for two or more years? Has it been in the same or a related field? Does the income fluctuate or is it consistent?

Income Type - What is the nature of the borrower's income? Is it wages, commission, or other? What is the frequency? Is it on a regular recurring schedule or is it seasonal? Is it bonus income tied to performance and therefore not guaranteed? If it is from a source other than traditional employment, how long will it continue?

Income amount - Is it adequate to cover the proposed new debt? Does the income show a pattern of decreasing or declining?

Capital - The capital that the borrower has on hand for down payment, closing costs, and/or reserves will impact your product choice. It will also impact underwriting. In the last module, we made note of the type of funds that are considered to be "**liquid assets**". In reviewing capital, consider them as the underwriter would:

Ownership - Does the borrower have full or limited access to the disclosed capital/assets? If not, what portion is available for the loan transaction?

Access/Liquidity - Are the funds liquid now or will they be soon? Is the borrower fully or partially vested? Are there penalties for withdrawal? Will the disbursement process be complete prior to the approval/rate lock expiration?

Amount - Is it enough to meet the requirements for down payment, closing costs, or cash reserves? Being able to answer the questions "Whose is it?" "How much is it?" and "When can they get it?" will help you evaluate your borrower's capital.

Conditions
- An underwriter looks at the many documents in the loan file to determine if there are any disclosed or undisclosed factors that might adversely affect the borrower or subject property. A few considerations include:

Employment at a place that has had a public announcement of shutting down.

A recently awarded divorce settlement where the borrower has to payout significant proceeds or will have a high **alimony/support payment.**

A lawsuit

An adverse **change in the industry** that the borrower is employed in

An adverse **change in the area** where the subject property is located

Collateral - A loan is secured using the subject property as collateral.

Since the property is the lender's protection against default, it must be structurally sound and functional. When evaluating the collateral, an underwriter considers:

Features -Are the features and style of the home consistent with what is available in the area?

Functionality -Is the home functional or has it been rendered obsolete by outdated features and capability.

Condition - Is the home structurally sound and visually appealing? Is the home inhabitable or is it a dangerous contraption. Is the home complete as is or will renovations be required?

Property type/Use - Is it residential or commercial? Is it owner occupied or is it a rental unit. Is it vacant or occupied?

After carefully and cautiously looking at all of these items and how they stack up to established guidelines. The underwriter should he able to confidently make a credit decision.

FINANCIAL FREEDOM

What does it take to achieve financial independence? Well, the truth is that there are and there have been many ways through which people have achieved financial freedom.

While success in the past might have come from social and political connections for instance, in today's business environment, success comes from taking advantage of today's better circumstances; you don't need to know anybody to excel in business! Let me explain:

The Ease of Starting a Business in Today's Business Environment

Many things have made starting a business easier than it has ever been; the development of technology is key among these things. More precisely, it is because of advancements in communication it is easier and convenient for businesses to connect and communicate with buyers. The internet has particularly made it easier to access information about anything. This is undeniably important in starting and managing any business.

Avenues such as mail, text, and instant messaging, video, live streaming, social media, and other budding tools have been among the most fascinating things technology has given the business world, giving it a major face lift.

Aspects of starting and conducting a business have radically changed. For instance, the way businesses engage in transactions and marketing to consumers has taken on a completely new life of its own. One of my friends described technology five years ago; he said, **"Technology is support brought to us by nature that we simply can't refuse. It makes it a lot easier to start a business and feel safe doing it.** "

Below are two of the numerous areas where we have experienced major changes in how we do business. We shall discuss them in detail so we can get a glimpse at what has changed.

The Internet

Twenty years ago, the widespread public use of the internet was still in its infancy. People were still getting over the wow-factor of building websites, using basic functions of the internet, learning new ideas, acquainting themselves with the use of email, and corporations were really competing to control the online marketplace. Google, Facebook, Amazon, and others emerged as central hubs of contemporary commerce in the digital domain.

Since then, we have seen the coming of age of technologies such as social bookmarking, social networking, search engine optimization, and other types of digital traffic generation. Today, these opportunities exist as a standard basis of operation in an enduring effort to grow sales volume on the internet.

The blogosphere, affiliate programs, and email lists that have auto-responders have come up as equally worthwhile avenues businesses can use to reach out and market to consumers. Currently, the internet has realized profits worth billions from the number of business transactions occurring online.

Modern business owners have a completely new perspective and outlook on marketing to consumers, and one demonstration of this is through the shift from traditional print advertisements and the ongoing efforts to create and develop company websites. The search for new ways to take advantage of the internet to produce new means of tapping into untapped online traffic continues.

POS Systems

A few decades ago, we had very little expertise on mobile payments or any experience with touch-screen product access especially in retail establishments. The emergence of modern **point of sale systems** (POS) has done a lot in offering modern retailers a great deal of benefit in optimizing their sales volume. By giving clients direct to on-site products and many payment options, POS systems make it cost effective and efficient to run a retail business.

Automation, a method that allows for inventory control measures, has completely revolutionized the current means of tracking and ordering inventory. Other developments such as mobile payments are still spreading fast.

New types of products have come into existence. Books are no longer the print books we used to have back in the days for instance; there are various digital versions of books (e-books), which are increasingly being consumed daily. This obviously requires a different method of product access and delivery to the customers (all done electronically), a phenomenon that has opened doors for limitless options on what someone can sell. Gone are the days when you could only stock physical goods when running a business- digital goods are taking over and presenting with them new forms of efficiency that allows businesses to run somewhat on autopilot and on minimal costs while targeting customers all over the world. That was unheard of in the past! What's even more interesting is **the way payments are processed**; it is just in ways many of us could not fathom a few years ago. You can receive payment from someone living in a different country without having to go to any bank and feel safe that your money is safe. The revolution of payments (which is automated) allows businesses to accept payment for goods and services day in day out from anywhere in the world (it doesn't matter whether their offices are closed- with a website and payment systems set, everything takes place seamlessly).

We could go on and on about how technology has developed because it evidently has, in hundreds of ways. **For instance**, because advances in communication have made it possible for information to travel quicker and more effectively, distance barriers have disappeared and many businesses are wholly exploiting options such as outsourcing overseas. Businesses can now outsource duties like telephone customer service, live chat, blog and article writing, and computer programming, and this is just but one of the numerous aspects of outsourcing. Moreover, businesses can now offer live support through a wide array of digital channels like mobile phones (Skype, WhatsApp etc.), live chat on their website, phone calls, social media and much more; the options are just limitless on how to reach out to past, current and potential customers to maximize sales and customer experience. Much of this can be done on the move; you don't need to be seated in an office to offer support; you could be out and about, at home, touring the world, in a different continent etc. , which essentially means you don't have to babysit the business to make it successful!

Technology has also made it **easier to seek help or support**. With the internet, the possibility of reaching hundreds of successful entrepreneurs and mentors is now possible through many platforms such as social media. By doing something as simple as typing words on the internet, you can reach many mentors who are willing to help startups in different and unique ways.

Many people out there have taken full advantage of the change we have today and the current opportunities to create wealth from entrepreneurship.

It is your prerogative to take advantage of the current state of affairs - the ease of doing business today; it has not always been like this!

A Stroll Down the Memory Lane: The Business Environment in Past

Let us take a trip down history and for comparison purposes, look at the state of doing business in the past.

First, in the past, there was a clear line between professional and private life. There were no phones, fancy tablets on which to check the stock market information at the comfort of your home, or laptops to carry work from your office to your house.

Before the 1990s, it was not easy to run business when you are away from it as we do today thanks to smartphones. Making calls outside payphones at gas stations was the norm and calling your employees or partners each time you had something new was obviously not easy back then.

It was even tougher getting work from different places; this is contrary to the online leads we have today. In 1994, there was a telemarketer. Business leads came through calls and perhaps referrals from a partner. Imagine that! It would take forever to grow, I imagine.

Globalization has also changed the business scene. In the past, only large businesses had the capacity to trade abroad. It was even more difficult to operate a business in more than one country.

In the past, licensing and other regulatory measures were tedious thanks in part to vexatious government bureaucratic tendencies that would make one hate themselves for thinking about starting his/her own business. At least today, governments have changed some policies and adopted others that make it easier to conduct business in multiple countries.

Because of a lack of efficient communication and other technology such as the internet, in the past, it was difficult to access support from experts or contact mentors. you would have to go through the trouble of meeting someone (usually marred by transport problems) to ask for technical help and guidance.

Looking at these things, you will undoubtedly agree with me when I say the internet has changed how entrepreneurs start and conduct business.

Nonetheless, things are not perfect, at least not for many people. Here is what I am talking about:

Doing Business Today: Modern Business Challenges

Even with the world having gone through massive changes such as those we have discussed - technology making it easy to start and manage businesses and expert mentors all over the world (often a click away) ready and willing to help - most of us are still not feeling confident or positive enough to start our businesses. For some, it is not a mere lack of confidence; they lack capital while others lack additional financial support from local lenders. They have very good business ideas but cannot implement them simply because they lack the funds to do so. Other people have enough capital but cannot lay out any good business idea.

I have personally met a few who have very good business ideas and the capital to start a business, but they never do so because **"they find it difficult to leave their corporate jobs. "** They also claim not to have enough time to start a business from scratch, or merely stick to the "**I think it's too late**" platitude.

This means that even with the world having changed, excuses, obstacles, and different kinds of pitfalls continue to exist; however, one thing is for sure, the starting-a-business challenges that may affect you today do not compare to those of starting a business in the past.

Who Wins & Who Loses

The truth is; it is much easier to start and grow a business to unfathomable levels than it is to climb the corporate ladder; there are many startups that are less than 5 years old that are averaging over a million dollars a year with very few employees to support the business. The question is; how long do you think it will take for your 9-5 to pay you a million dollars or even half of it? You decide!

Even with the current opportunities; there will be winners and losers in life. The winners are those that will choose to take the leap of faith and start taking action as far as starting their own businesses goes (you don't have to quit your day job!) and losers will be those who decide to play safe.

With me acting as your guide through the maze of everything you need to know in respect to starting a successful business, I believe you will see things differently and take full advantage of the currently existing favorable business environment even when it has its fair share of obstacles you will undoubtedly have to tackle.

The solution to every obstacle is often simple. It only requires that we change how we think, and ultimately, how we do things because we have to realize that we are working in a rat race kind of world. It is impossible to imagine the joy that comes with knowing we are trying to escape this race and are **making more money, working less hours** on our terms, meanwhile making a difference in people's lives.

START by changing the thought that working hard at our day jobs - usually in the corporate sector - is all we need to make it in life or is the easier option to achieving our ambitions and financial freedom.

With my little wealth of experience, I have realized that working hard for somebody else is like the proverbial **hamster wheel** for many people. You work round the clock, and your rewards (compared to your work value), which may be just above peanuts, never seem to be enough and a promotion is never a guarantee.

I can still recall a close friend telling me that after she started thinking about starting a business of her own, she would quickly dismiss the ideas simply because she lacked confidence to pursue that dream.

One day, she went to one of her directors with a load of ideas about how to increase productivity in her company by streamlining the sales department. The director only turned to her and said softly, "**the day you become a director of your own company is the day you get to implement this.** " She said that it was in that moment that she decided to start her own company, and she did.

She went into the corporate world because of her high ambition; she also wanted money and respect. She worked her way up only to find out the truth about the **'glass ceiling.** ' She was working up to 80 hours per week for peanuts.

Starting your own business is the only guaranteed path to financial freedom. It worked for my lady-friend (she now owns a therapy complex) and it will undoubtedly work for you.

She merely followed simple rules that people who win, or rather, people who make it and become wealthy follow. **The people who win at life and business are those that:**

- **Desire to start early** so that they can gain enough experience and in good time.
- **Have the passion** to learn the ins and outs of a business.
- **Are eager fast learners and observers**; if they are not fast learners, they are willing to do whatever it takes to learn.
- Know how to **adapt to any given situation** because they have their eyes firmly on the prize.
- Strive to achieve **continuous personal development** at all levels.
- **Seek mentors** and do not necessarily try to reinvent the

wheel. They listen to the experts and make good wise decisions based on expert guidance.

- **Seek help of like-minded individuals.** In the world of business, no man is an island.

As for the losers, those who lose even with the opportunities that exist today are those:

- People who are **too proud or afraid** to try new things.
- People who are lazy, and **don't have sense of personal responsibility.**
- People who are **unobservant.**
- Who are **close minded**
- Who **refuse to learn** and read books, attend seminars.
- Who think **they know everything already.**

START YOUR JOURNEY TO FINANCIAL FREEDOM

The concept of time and money had changed throughout history. The term Financial Freedom has gained much popularity in the ever changing financial scenario today. More and more people are on the lookout for home based business ideas and opportunities. If you'll browse the internet, there are tons of programs online which offer top home business ideas and home business reviews.

TIME IS MONEY
All of us have one thing in common - TIME. A well-known celebrity, a famous author or an ordinary person all have 24 hours to spend in a day.

More often, we exchange our time for money. Day in and day out, we spend 12 hours or more at work in order for us to earn wages. We work extra hard but still not able to achieve the financial freedom we strive for.

Financial freedom enables a person to have time freedom - enjoying life without hampering his steady income in any manner. This is based on managing assets and investments that are compounded over time to generate steady flow of cash.

It can be achieved. We just need to continuously learn new ways which will guide us towards our journey. We must make a plan and work hard to accomplish that plan. Here are 7 tips which can help you on your journey to financial freedom

1.) You are who you think you are...

How you see yourself determines how successful you will become. The journey starts when we embrace "**Change**". We must re-calibrate the way we think. We were told that in order for us to earn money, we must work hard.

Once upon a time, there was a **Donkey** which fell in a deep pit. He tried so hard to climb out of the hole but to no avail. Then finally, he stopped realizing that his efforts are not doing him any good. The donkey kept telling himself "**there is a better way... there is a better way**".

The owner, thinking that there is no hope for the donkey, decided to bury him to die in the deep pit. He started throwing dirt into the pit. The donkey felt the dirt thrown on his back. Immediately, he closed his eyes, shook the dirt off, and stepped back. He went on with this until the hole was filled with dirt, and he was able to step out towards his freedom.

Just like the donkey, we must **start looking at ALL things positively**. **The dirt** symbolizes the negative things happening in our lives. We call them trials. Our success is determined by how we look at those trials and how well we react to them. We must always have a positive mindset, whether in our families or towards earning money. A healthy perception of money is necessary in order to maintain an over-all balance.

Focus on making, money work for you, instead of you working for money. Remember that you earn money in order to achieve your ends. .

2.) Your Health is Your Greatest Wealth...

We've all heard the phrase - Health is Wealth. Your health is your greatest wealth. Do you think you will have REAL FREEDOM if you're financially free but you're too sick to enjoy it? We want to be financially free so that we can have more time to do the most important things in life - Family, Community, etc.

You should look at your health as your greatest asset. Follow these 3 tips for a healthier you...

- Do have **periodic check-ups** with your physician. Do not self-medicate. It is best to get opinion from experts when it comes to your health.

- Do **regular exercises.** Work to achieve your desired heart rate per day. You'll discover that physical activities condition your body and you'll can delivery both physically and mentally to complete the task at hand.

- **Watch your diet**. You are what you eat. A good diet can boost both your mental and physical being to be able to achieve what you want in life.

3.) Know What You Want...

Will you leave home without knowing where you are going? Similarly, you will not be able to start your journey towards financial freedom if you don't know what you really want.

This is the most important activity that you need to do if you want to reach your goals. Your vision is the most important factor of your success. You should define what you want to achieve at the beginning of your journey to financial freedom. What do you want to achieve? Why do you want to achieve these? You have to answer these questions as you are developing your vision.

When you have done the above mentioned, follow these simple steps:

- **Write down your vision or dreams.** Put in the details that you want.

- **Read and imagine this vision every day.** It is vital to **"feel"** these visions coming true in your mind. This way, you'll start believing and you'll start achieving. **What your mind can conceive, and your heart believes, your body can achieve.**

- **strengthen your will to achieve.** There may be obstacles along the way but you'll be very focused that you'll find a way around those obstacles.

4.) Earn As Much As You Can...

The best way to fail in your journey is to have only one income stream. It is like being dependent on one water source for all you needs. What happens if the river runs dry? The whole community will thirst.

All of us should strive to have multiple streams of income. The number of income streams that we have will determine how fast we can achieve our financial goals.

Do a research on how to build multiple income streams. It is best to look for ways to build multiple streams of passive income. The internet offers a variety of top home business ideas and opportunities. Although we've heard that the net is full of scammers, there are still legitimate home business opportunities available. You must do extensive research for top home business ideas. You can Google the terms **"work from home on the internet"** or **"How to start an internet business."**

5.) Save As Much As You Can...

Always strive to save a part of your earnings before you make any spending. This way, you are paying yourself first by paying your savings account first. There are various vehicles where we can put the money, savings account, time deposits, mutual funds, investing directly on the stock market or investing in your own business.

The most ideal is to save 20% of your earning and **put it in**

various investment vehicles. This way, you are assured that your money will grow and earn for you passive income. Always research where to your money will earn faster. Be wary though, there are still scammers out there waiting to take hold of your hard-earned cash.

As the saying goes - "**Save in the spring so you won't beg in the fall**".

6.) Simplify Your Life As Much As You Can...

When you have money, you can afford to buy so many things. In fact, you'll be tempted to buy things **that are not that important in your life.**

BEWARE!!!

There are more important things in life than material things. Simplifying your life means you'll get detached from material possessions. This will enable us to focus more on our relationships rather than special gadgets and expensive toy.

Differentiate between your wants and your needs. If you don't need it, don't buy it.

Simple living creates a space in our hearts which enables us to enjoy even the very little things in life. Material possessions will only complicate things.

We will learn to love and serve the "**Real People**" around us instead of the "**Reel people**" we see in our flat screen TV. We will enjoy nature's music more than the song we'll hear in our audio surround system.

7.) Love More...

Real financial freedom lies in the relationship we have with other people. It is having the time to serve and love people more and more each day.

True wealth is found in relationships. We know that all of us have limited amount of time here in this world. One day, that time will end. And on our deathbed, what will matter most is our relationship with the people around us. **We don't look for our Ferrari, or our Home theater system or the cash we have in the bank.** Instead, we want our love ones - family, relatives, and friends - to spend their time with us.

How often do we hear the words "**If only I had spent more time with him**," or "**If only I hug him one more time**", during wakes and funerals? At the end of our journey here, still what matters most is the time we've spent with our loved ones.

Friend, don't wait till it's over. Do it now. Love more each day.

The journey to financial freedom requires commitment and determination. Rest assured, there will be difficulties along the way. The challenges are there to mold our characters, not to keep us down. Always focus on our goal no matter what lies ahead.

Go on my friend. Start your journey to financial freedom. Keep focused. And when you reach your goal, you will look back and tell yourself - well done.

THE 6 KEYS TO FINANCIAL FREEDOM

To gain financial freedom, you need a financial plan to keep you focused.

Financial freedom comes from creating a nest egg of assets that can support your lifestyle with passive income.

There are 6 key steps to Financial Freedom :
- Set your goals
- Pay your self first
- Utilise compound interest
- Protect your assets
- Asset Allocation/Diversification
- Leverage or Gearing

1. Set your Goals:

Financial Freedom is a journey from where you are today, to where you want to be in the future. Like any destination, if you don't know where you are going, it sure is hard deciding what is best today to hit that target.

In 1953 a Harvard University study, **noted only 10% of the class had goals,** with only 3% having them written down. On reviewing the situation in 1973 - **the 10% with goals had achieved more wealth than the other 90% combined** and were also **healthier and happier.**

So what are you waiting for - write down those goals, something magical might start to happen

2. Pay your self first:

Have you ever noticed when you get a raise at work, that you still can't save anything? Suddenly everything costs more just when the wage increase hits the bank account. What ever we are left with in our pay each week, we adjust our livestyle to need all the new pay as well. Taking a percentage out of the pay before it is credited to your bank account is a sure way of looking after yourself. If you spend everything before next payday, oh well better luck next week.

The State/Government understands our purchasing habits. That is why Tax is taken out by the employer as **Pay as You Go** (PAYE) and sent directly to the tax department. Stand up and be as important as the Government in your life and pay your self first as well. Ask your pay clerk if they can put a percentage of your wages into a special long term savings account.

3. Compound Interest;

Compound interest is magical - it is the 8th wonder of the world. This is where you get interest paid on your savings, let the interest buildup and then get interest on the original sum + the interest.

Watching your investment grow **requires patience and discipline.**

There is an investment rule called - **the rule of 72.** If you were to get 7.2% interest on your $1000-00 every year (and left the interest to grow with the original sum). In 10 years your investment would be $2000-00. What the rule says - if you divide the interest rate into 72, the answer is the number of years it takes for the investment to double (with the interest compounding)

Time is the friend of compound interest. If you put $10,000 away when you were 25 years at a compounded interest rate of 7.2% how much would it grow to by age 65 ? *

4. Protect your assets

What is your most valuable asset ? Do you think it is your house, or maybe your car ?

It is easy to see the physical assets (or are they liabilities) that we own.

Your ability to earn an income is your most important asset. This is a vital part of financial planning and wealth creation to achieve Financial Freedom. If you are 30 years old and earn $40,000 per year, your earning capacity is $1,200,000 - **YOU ARE A POTENTIAL MILLIONAIRE.** It is how much your end up keeping that makes the difference in the end.

You can protect your income through income protection insurance. Insurance companies offer different conditions and it is important to read carefully how they define " loss of earning" The 3 greatest life time risks are:

- **Becoming disabled**
- **Dying too soon**
- **Living too long**

Refer to the Insurance Section to see an overview of the risks that could disrupt your journey toward Financial Freedom. To fully evaluate you own risk circumstances contact your Insurance adviser who can do a Risk Management Plan to assess what best fits your situation.

5. Asset Allocation

In 1930, the US President asked the US Securities Commission to investigate how to avoid a future financial crisis that had occurred in 1929 with the share market crash on Wall Street. The Cowles Commission was formed. The 4 key conclusions from the commission are:

- Buy quality
- Diversify
- Hire Professional Fund Managers
- Dollar Cost Average

Asset allocation is fundamental to maximising your investment strategy within your investment time frame. The main asset classes are **cash, fixed interest, property and shares**. All these assets have different returns and risks associated with them. Cash is mare predictable in the short term. Shares need a longer time frame to move through the economic cycles. Diversification is selecting across the four asset class to spread your risk. We often say don't put all your eggs in one basket

6. Leverage / Gearing

There are different ways to leverage an asset. You can leverage an asset, such as a house, shares, investments or income. Leverage is where you take on extra risk and borrow against the asset to purchase a higher priced asset. Leveraging your income is where you borrow money to make investments and use the excess income to pay off the debt. **Leverage can increase your wealth exponentially in a favourable market, or increase your losses dramatically in unfavourable times.** Leverage and equity structures can be tax efficient, and specific advice must be sort from a Tax Specialist to assess your own specific circumstances. This article is not specific in regards to tax, and is commenting at a general level only as different country jurisdictions can vary .

www.ingramcontent.com/pod-product-compliance
Lightning Source LLC
Chambersburg PA
CBHW070653220526
45466CB00001B/416